THE
ILLUSTRATED HISTORY OF WEAPONS
PISTOLS

KINGSFORDEDITIONS

Distributed by Kingsford Editions
45–55 Fairchild Street
Heatherton Victoria 3202 Australia
www.hinkler.com.au

Created by Moseley Road Inc.
President: Sean Moore
Project art and editorial director: Lisa Purcell
Cover and internal design: Hinkler Design Studio
Photographer: Jonathan Conklin Photography, Inc.
f-stop fitzgerald
Author: Rupert Matthews
Prepress: Graphic Print Group

ISBN: 978 1 7436 3056 3

Printed and bound in China

THE
ILLUSTRATED HISTORY OF WEAPONS
PISTOLS

Chuck Wills

KINGSFORD EDITIONS

Contents

French Pepperbox
(See page 62)

Introduction:
A Weapon of Skill

To describe a pistol as a "handheld firearm" is accurate, but it fails to capture the importance of this weapon to the world. It was the pistol that for the first time made personal combat a matter of skill rather than of strength or stamina. Combatants may have needed skill to effectively wield swords, knives, axes and other older types of weapons, but they also needed muscles and brute strength. The pistol needs only skill—and maybe a steady hand.

The First Pistols

The very first pistols emerged more than five centuries ago as the earliest gunsmiths began to realize that their products could be made small enough to be held in the hand, and yet remain effective weapons. Like all medieval firearms, those early weapons were crude, inaccurate and temperamental. Sometimes they fired, sometimes they didn't. Over the years gunsmiths worked hard to produce a handheld firearm that would work when it was needed.

The early advances were basic, but fundamental. Gunpowder that needed to be remixed just before it was used was replaced by milled powder that remained stable in the long term and needed only to be put into a gun to be effective. The ironworking skills need to produce barrels that could withstand the explosive forces of a gun being fired time after time were gradually developed. Thus weapons that could be relied upon not to burst with catastrophic results could be made light enough to be held in one hand.

EARLY GUNSMITHS

Dating from the 17th century, each illustration in this series of manuscript illuminations depicts a gunsmith at work.

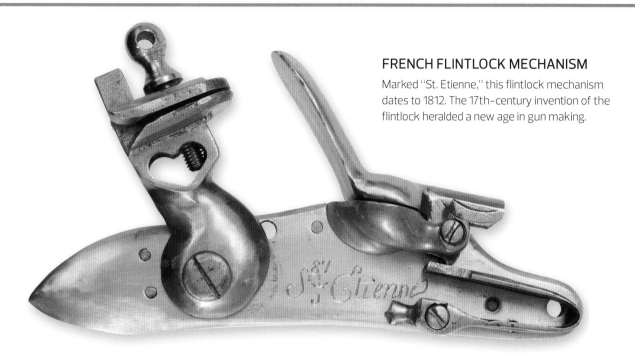

FRENCH FLINTLOCK MECHANISM
Marked "St. Etienne," this flintlock mechanism dates to 1812. The 17th-century invention of the flintlock heralded a new age in gun making.

Much more difficult to solve was the problem of making the weapon fire. The first method was to drill a small hole in the rear of the muzzle. Sticking a hot wire or burning coal in the hole set off the gunpowder in the weapon. Neither of these methods worked in rainy or windy weather, though, and in any case, having a naked flame in the presence of gunpowder was not a good idea, as far too many people found out to their cost.

QUEEN ANNE PISTOL
A Queen Anne pistol by Turvey of London is decorated with fine silver filigree. In Queen Anne flintlock pistols the lockplate is forged in one piece with the breech and the trigger plate.

From Matchlock to Flintlock

The matchlock of the 16th century went some way to solving the problems of triggering the gun—quite literally in one sense because it was the matchlock that first introduced a trigger mechanism to the pistol. The later wheel lock was rather more effective, though more costly. It was the flintlock invented in the early 17th century that first gave the pistol a reasonably reliable method of being discharged.

Through the 17th and 18th centuries, gunsmiths developed a range of pistols for different purposes. Using the flintlock, they produced pocket pistols for personal protection, dragons to deter bandits or to be taken into battle, and long-barreled holster pistols for cavalry troops.

Flintlocks were also the mechanism for the dainty, exquisitely beautiful and excessively deadly specialist dueling pistols that took the lives of many a proud young gentleman.

The Industrial Revolution

It was the invention in the 19th century of fulminating compounds that will detonate when hit hard enough that really caused the pistol to come of age. When put into a metal jacket along with a main propellant charge and the bullet, the fulminating compounds produced the familiar modern cartridge. These metal cartridges were robust, reliable and increasingly inexpensive to manufacture.

Pistol makers had already experimented with methods of allowing a pistol to fire more than once without being reloaded. Having more than one barrel worked for a while, but then was replaced by a single barrel backed by a number of bullets held in a rotating cylinder. These revolvers were finally made effective by the metallic cartridge.

SAMUEL COLT MEMORIAL

Erected in Colt Park, Hartford, Connecticut, where Samuel Colt founded Colt's Patent Firearms Manufacturing Company, this statue pays tribute to the firearm inventor and industrialist. Colt's work was instrumental in making the mass production of the revolver commercially viable.

Semiautomatics and Beyond

If the metal cartridge made the revolver a really useful weapon in battle, on the frontier or for personal protection, it also made possible an entirely new form of pistol. The semiautomatic pistol had a self-loading mechanism that allowed bullets to be drawn up from a magazine into the firing chamber and barrel without the user needing to do anything other than pull the trigger.

This book traces the history of the pistol from its early crude origins through numerous forms and guises to its modern-day face as a personal protection weapon for soldiers, police, civilians and criminals alike. The pistol emerges as an archetypal weapon that has helped to shape the world—for good and for bad—but a tool of mankind that has never been more useful or widely used than it is today.

POLICE PISTOLS

Since World War II, the trend has been for semiautomatics to replace the standard-issue revolvers usually used by the armed forces. Although the transition has been slower, the same is true for police and law enforcement.

DOUBLE-BARRELED DERRINGER

Made in 1887, this derringer (shown open) was made as a pocket pistol. The small size of derringers made them perfect choices for women, who could hide them in a purse or muff.

.44 MAGNUM CARTRIDGE

Metallic cartridges revolutionized the making of pistols. Shown here is a .44 Magnum cartridge with a 9mm bullet.

Early Firearms

Handheld Gunpowder Weapons

Holding a gunpowder weapon in your hand was an inherently dangerous thing to do. Early firearms were prone to explode when fired; a notable victim was King James II of Scotland, who was killed in this way at the siege of Roxburgh in 1460. Nevertheless, by around 1450, all armies in Europe and Asia included troops armed with handheld guns. These early weapons were extremely effective, and developments to barrel design, projectile and, crucially, the firing mechanism followed over the next five centuries. By the mid-19th century the pistol was a fully formed modern weapon ready to take the next great leap forward in technology.

SOLDIERS OF THE BURGUNDIAN WARS. During the early 15th century the dukes of Burgundy sought to become independent of the kingdom of France, launching a series of devastating wars. The Burgundians were noted for their innovative use of firearms and novel tactics.

The Matchlock Mechanism

The very first guns were fired by pushing a piece of coal or heated iron wire into the touch hole, thus setting off the gun. Such a system was rather hit or miss and was effectively impossible to use in rain.

By the end of the 15th century, a new device called a matchlock had been developed. Acting as a match, a length of cord soaked in saltpeter was set alight and would smolder reliably for over an hour. A lever on the side of the gun had the match clamped at one end. When the bottom end of the lever was pulled back, the top end moved forward to push the match into the touch hole and fire the gun. To this day, this simple device is the reason why gun triggers are under the barrel and pull backward.

A matchlock mechanism

FRENCH HAND GONNE

This "hand gonne" dates to about 1450 and was operated by a two-man team. Both men would mix the gunpowder and load the weapon. Then, while one man held the wooden block on to which the barrel is fixed, the other would push a coal or wire into the touch hole. The caliber of the barrel is about an inch.

BATTLE OF MORAT GUN

On the morning of June 22, 1476, a sudden heavy shower of rain deluged the ranks of the Burgundian army camped around the Swiss city of Morat. This effectively rendered the famous Burgundian firearms useless. When the Swiss attacked an hour later with pikes, halberds and swords, they smashed the Burgundian army to pieces. The Duke of Burgundy's baggage fell into Swiss hands, and much of it is still on display at nearby Guyere Castle. Among the loot was this simple, one-piece handgun, the shape of which foreshadows that of later pistols.

SPANISH HAND CANNON

One of the earliest weapons that could be classed as a pistol is this 15th-century gun from Spain. Although officially designated a "hand cannon" it has no wooden base with which to brace it under the arm or against the chest. Instead the lion forms a handle to be held in one hand while the weapon is fired.

JAPANESE PISTOL

From 1633 to 1853 Japan cut itself off from the outside world, with death the penalty for any person who entered or left the country. Before the policy began, Japan had imported some matchlock weapons from Europe, and local gunsmiths continued to produce copies during the years of isolation. This particular weapon has a simple stud trigger, operated by squeezing it into the butt. The metal clip on the side of the weapon was designed to be slipped into a belt for easy carrying.

The ornate decoration on the Chinese signal gun indicates that it was to be used by a high status commander, not a humble soldier.

CHINESE SIGNAL GUN

Although it dates to the 18th century, this device is of a design that was already two centuries old. This is a small gun that was used to send signals rather than to fire bullets. The noise of the discharge was used to send a predetermined signal to distant troops. This Chinese signal gun is made of bronze, which was less prone to bursting or failure than was contemporary iron.

The Wheel Lock

A key problem with the matchlock was that it involved soldiers holding a spluttering match while pouring out gunpowder—with inevitable dangers. What was needed was a system that created sparks when the trigger was pulled, not before. The first answer was the wheel lock, developed about 1500. This device had several moving parts powered by a spring. When the trigger was pulled the spring-loaded steel wheel began spinning. At the same moment a piece of pyrite was pushed against the teeth of the wheel. The friction of steel on pyrite created a shower of sparks. Simultaneously a cover was lifted off a flat pan on which had been sprinkled some gunpowder.

The sparks ignited the gunpowder, the resulting flash traveling through the touch hole to fire the pistol.

The mechanism was delicate and costly to make, and was also slower to use, as the user not only had to load the barrel but also prime the pan and wind up the spring. As a consequence the wheel lock never completely replaced the much cheaper and more robust matchlock. The fact that the wheel-lock pistol could be kept in a pocket, then produced and fired made it a favorite weapon of assassins. Among those killed by such a weapon were William the Silent of the Netherlands (1584), the Duke of Guise (1563) and Admiral Coligny (1572).

ENGLISH WHEEL-LOCK PISTOL

An unusual English wheel-lock pistol from the later 16th century. Note that it has two triggers, each operating a separate mechanism, thus reducing the chances of a misfire. The short barrel meant this was a relatively inaccurate weapon, even for its day.

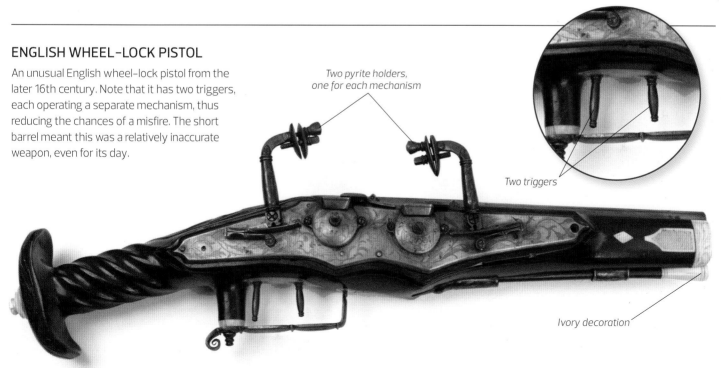

Two pyrite holders, one for each mechanism

Two triggers

Ivory decoration

GUSTAVUS ADOLPHUS OF SWEDEN

One of the foremost military leaders of the 17th century, King Gustavus Adolphus of Sweden was shot in the shoulder with a pistol during a skirmish in 1627. The bullet lodged under the shoulder blade and could not be removed. This made it impossible for him to wear armor over his shoulder, a fact that caused his death in battle at Lützen in 1632. He was noted for his skilful handling of combined arms, particularly the way cavalry armed with pistol and sword cooperated with musket- and pike-armed infantry.

GERMAN WHEEL-LOCK PISTOLS

A beautiful pair of wheel-lock pistols heavily decorated in ivory and made in Saxony around 1590. The metal prong is, in fact, the key that was used to wind up the wheel-lock mechanism. The decorated box held five pre-prepared cartridges, consisting of a bullet and a measured amount of gunpowder wrapped in a tube of paper. The heavy ball at the end of the handle was intended to be used as a weapon. Once the pistol had been fired, the owner held it by the barrel and used it as a club.

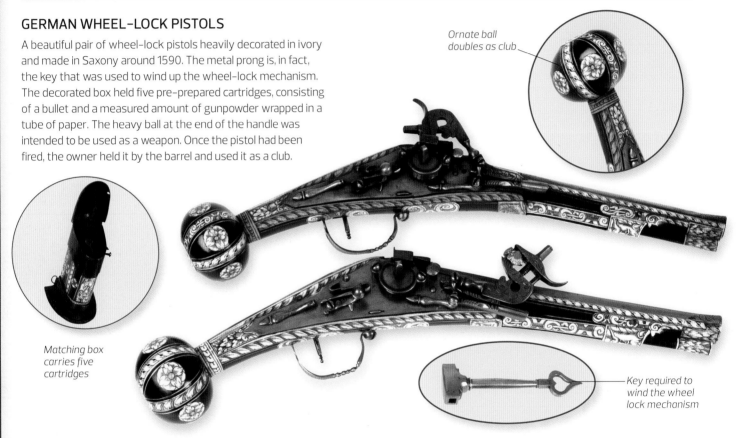

Ornate ball doubles as club

Matching box carries five cartridges

Key required to wind the wheel lock mechanism

RAMPART GUN

Rampart guns were designed to be placed in hidden settings in fortifications, usually where no man could possibly be concealed. They were operated by means of a string or wire that was pulled when an enemy unwittingly came into the line of fire. This example has a caliber of .76 inch and may have fired shot rather than a single bullet.

The Flintlock

Good as the wheel lock was, it had the disadvantages of a complex mechanism and high cost. A cheaper, more reliable alternative came in the form of the flintlock, which was developed about 1610 and remained the main method of firing guns well into the 19th century.

The flintlock operates with a relatively simple mechanism powered by a spring. The key innovation proved to be the frizzen: a metal extension of the pan cover that curves up and back from the rear of the pan cover. Once the gun is loaded, the cock is pulled back, which puts the spring under tension. When the trigger is pulled, the cock is jerked forward by the spring. As it does so the cock pushes the flint into the frizzen at an angle. This pushes the frizzen forward, lifting the pan cover and exposing the powder. At the same time the flint scrapes along the frizzen, creating a shower of sparks that falls onto the powder and ignites it.

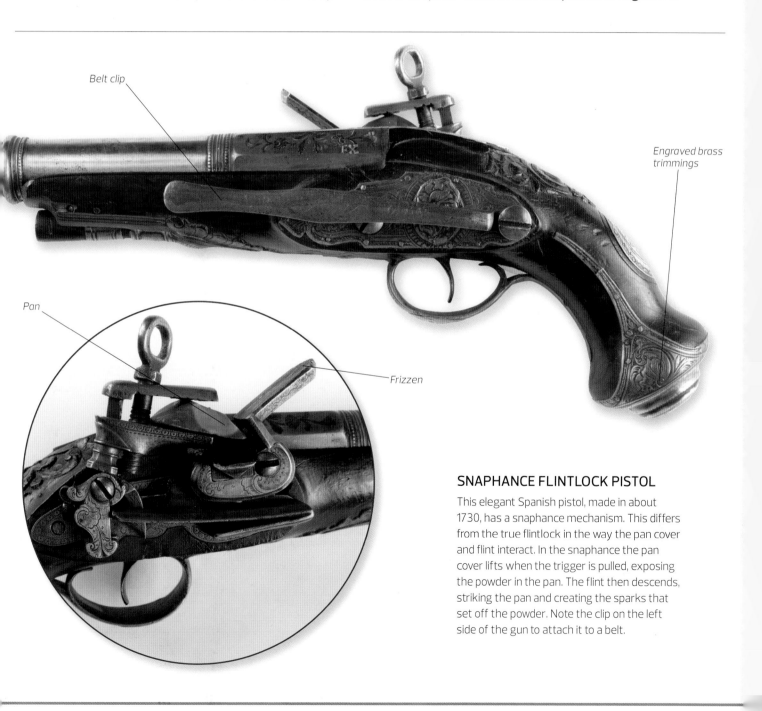

Belt clip

Engraved brass trimmings

Pan

Frizzen

SNAPHANCE FLINTLOCK PISTOL

This elegant Spanish pistol, made in about 1730, has a snaphance mechanism. This differs from the true flintlock in the way the pan cover and flint interact. In the snaphance the pan cover lifts when the trigger is pulled, exposing the powder in the pan. The flint then descends, striking the pan and creating the sparks that set off the powder. Note the clip on the left side of the gun to attach it to a belt.

COAT, BELT AND HOLSTER PISTOLS

During the course of the 18th century pistols came to be categorized into three rough classes, based on their use rather than any difference in operation.

Coat pistols were those with short—sometimes very short—barrels. They were personal defense weapons kept in pockets or bags and effective only at very close quarters. Coat pistols tended to have smooth, rounded shapes so that they did not snag on clothing.

Belt pistols were larger and came with a metal clip to attach them to belts. The barrels were longer, making these weapons effective at up to 30 feet or so.

The largest pistols were holster pistols, which were designed to be carried in holsters attached to a horse saddle. These not only had the longest barrels, but they were also bigger, heavier guns that could be used as clubs in a fight.

CLERMONT PISTOL

A small pistol made in France with a stamp reading "a Clermont" on the lock plate. It is a finely made weapon with an octagonal base to the barrel and a round muzzle engraved with lines. Note the metal knob on the butt, which may have been intended to be used as a knuckleduster-type weapon if the bullet failed to do its job.

Metal knob

Stamp reading "a Clermont"

Flint in down position

FRENCH COAT PISTOL

Made in France around the year 1800, this snub-nosed coat pistol is a plain weapon with a wooden butt and minimum of decoration. The flint, shown here in the down position, has the typically pointed wedge shape that was required if it was to produce a good shower of sparks when it hit the frizzen.

FOUR-BARRELED PEPPERBOX PISTOL

This unusual weapon, made in France about the year 1820, has four rifled barrels operated by two flintlock mechanisms. Each trigger operates one of the cocks, firing one of the upper barrels. Once the two upper barrels have been fired, the barrel assembly is twisted 180 degrees to bring the bottom barrels to the top, ready to be fired. This system of rotating barrels is known as the "pepperbox."

Taps for each vertical pair

The grooves along the barrels were an early form of rifling.

BLACKBEARD THE PIRATE

Edward Teach, an English pirate active in the Caribbean in the early 18th century, was notorious for his daring, ruthlessness and cruelty. Teach is better known by the nickname "Blackbeard," acquired because of his luxurious jet-black beard. He habitually went into battle armed with a cutlass and four pistols, while he tucked burning matches into his hat to swathe himself in sulphurous smoke. On one occasion he shot his first mate, Israel Hands, in the leg with a flintlock pistol, declaring if he did not shoot one of his crew from time to time they would forget who he was!

Key Guns

Key guns were first developed in the late 16th century and remained in use until the early 19th century. As their name suggests, they were a combination of a key and a gun. This type of gun was developed in case a jailer or watchman needed to guard himself against a surprise attack and so needed a gun that was immediately at hand at all times. It has been suggested that a key gun could even be fired when the key was in the lock of the door, sending the bullet through to the other side of the door. The practicality of this combination has been called into question, however. The rough handling that a key gets in everyday use makes it unlikely that the gun could be kept loaded at all times. Moreover, the key part of many of the key guns that survive look barely used. It may be that the key gun was more useful as a threat than as a real weapon.

ENGLISH KEY GUN

This key gun was made in England in about 1810. The pivoting lever just in front of the key handle is the trigger, which, when pulled, fires a bullet down the shank. It is thought that this might be a gun disguised to look like a key rather than a true key gun.

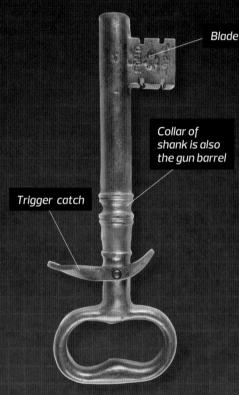

Blade

Collar of shank is also the gun barrel

Trigger catch

Pan

Engraved hammer

Barrel and key shank as one

Trigger guard

Key bit acts as the muzzle

PERCUSSION–CAP KEY GUN

This weapon belongs to the mid-19th century and has a conventional percussion-cap mechanism. The handle is flat-sided wood set into a steel frame. The key element was welded on to the barrel and was individually made for the customer's lock.

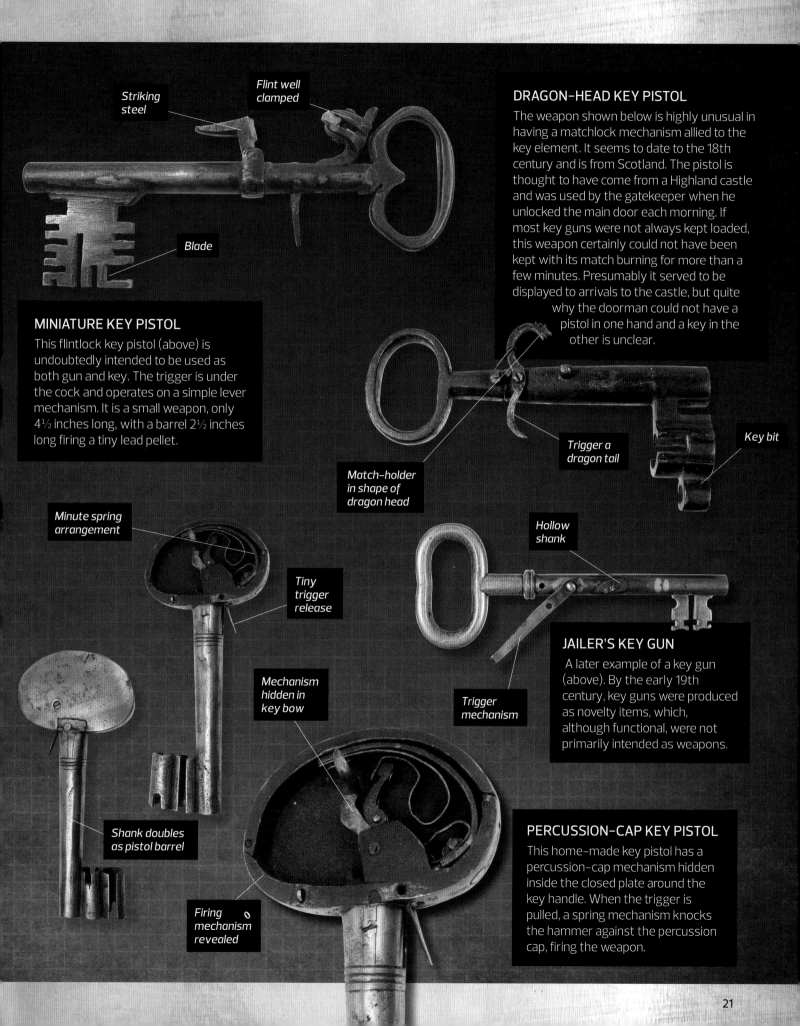

Striking steel

Flint well clamped

Blade

MINIATURE KEY PISTOL

This flintlock key pistol (above) is undoubtedly intended to be used as both gun and key. The trigger is under the cock and operates on a simple lever mechanism. It is a small weapon, only 4½ inches long, with a barrel 2½ inches long firing a tiny lead pellet.

DRAGON-HEAD KEY PISTOL

The weapon shown below is highly unusual in having a matchlock mechanism allied to the key element. It seems to date to the 18th century and is from Scotland. The pistol is thought to have come from a Highland castle and was used by the gatekeeper when he unlocked the main door each morning. If most key guns were not always kept loaded, this weapon certainly could not have been kept with its match burning for more than a few minutes. Presumably it served to be displayed to arrivals to the castle, but quite why the doorman could not have a pistol in one hand and a key in the other is unclear.

Match-holder in shape of dragon head

Trigger a dragon tail

Key bit

Minute spring arrangement

Tiny trigger release

Mechanism hidden in key bow

Hollow shank

Trigger mechanism

Shank doubles as pistol barrel

JAILER'S KEY GUN

A later example of a key gun (above). By the early 19th century, key guns were produced as novelty items, which, although functional, were not primarily intended as weapons.

Firing mechanism revealed

PERCUSSION-CAP KEY PISTOL

This home-made key pistol has a percussion-cap mechanism hidden inside the closed plate around the key handle. When the trigger is pulled, a spring mechanism knocks the hammer against the percussion cap, firing the weapon.

Flintlock mechanism

Brass barrel

Brass grip

BRASS FLINTLOCK PISTOLS

This pair of weapons are highly unusual in that the butt and barrel of the pistols are made of brass instead of the usual wood. Made in France in the 18th century, these extraordinary flintlock pistols are long and slender with long, pointed grips that might also have been used as weapons.

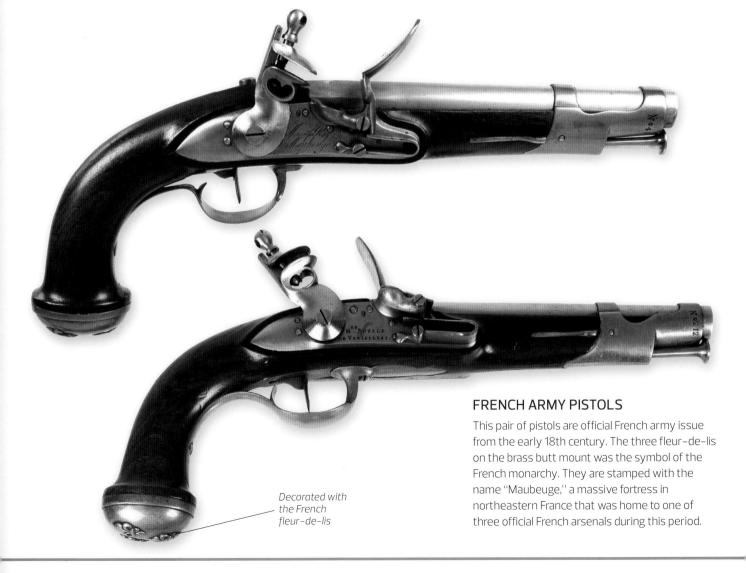

FRENCH ARMY PISTOLS

This pair of pistols are official French army issue from the early 18th century. The three fleur-de-lis on the brass butt mount was the symbol of the French monarchy. They are stamped with the name "Maubeuge," a massive fortress in northeastern France that was home to one of three official French arsenals during this period.

Decorated with the French fleur-de-lis

GEORGE WASHINGTON

The first president of the United States, George Washington was born in Virginia in 1732. Washington grew up on his family plantation and at the age of 21 became an officer in the Virginia militia. Part of the standard equipment of a militia officer during this period was a pair of holster flintlock pistols attached to the saddle along with a sword, and many chose to carry a musket as well.

By the time Washington had risen to command the American forces in the Revolutionary War against Britain, he had, like most senior commanders of his day, dispensed with his firearms and retained only a sword of mostly ceremonial use.

FLINTLOCK TRAP GUN

This weapon was made by Heinrich Kappell, a famous Danish gunsmith who was active from 1674 to 1718. There is no trigger guard and the rudimentary handle has a hole through it from top to bottom. This marks this weapon as a "trap gun," used for hunting. The gun was fixed to a post through the hole in its butt and the trigger was connected by a string or wire to a tripwire or hinged plate. When an animal triggered the tripwire or trod on the plate, the wire pulled the trigger and fired the gun, which was aimed at where the animal would be standing.

Flintlock mechanism

Guardless trigger

TURN-OFFS AND TURNOVERS

The flintlock mechanism was simple and effective, but it suffered from the fact that the weapon was slow to reload and fiddly to prepare for firing. Moreover, the gun needed to be held the right way up or the powder in the pan might fall out. This all meant that a pistol was useless once fired until it went through the lengthy reloading process. Numerous methods were developed to make flintlock pistols quicker to reload in a combat situation, the most common of which were the "turn-off" and the "turnover" systems.

A turn-off pistol had a barrel that could be either unscrewed or unclipped. A prepared paper cartridge could then be pushed into the breech end of the barrel, which was then repositioned ready for firing. This system was often used in pistols with a rifled barrel, as hammering a ball down the grooves of the barrel could be time consuming.

The turnover model took a different approach. Several different barrels were each loaded in turn. When the pistol had been fired, the barrels were rotated so that a new barrel was put into position by the flintlock mechanism.

The turn-off and the turnover systems were both reasonably effective ways to increase the rate of fire. Still, problems remained, including issues firing the gun in the rain and fouling of the barrel by powder residues.

ITALIAN PISTOLS

These two pistols were produced in the early 19th century in Turin, capital of the kingdom of Sardinia and home to the royal dynasty of Italy. This major European capital was also one of the first Italian cities to industrialize, and led the industrial revolution in the Mediterranean. These little pistols have hardwood stocks and brass mountings, indicating their superior quality.

DUCKFOOT PISTOL

This unusual pistol was made in London around 1800 by Goodwin & Co. The pattern of radiating barrels is known as the duckfoot due to its resemblance to the webbed foot of a duck. Each barrel is of .45 caliber and fired a single lead ball, and all barrels were fired simultaneously by the same flintlock. The intimidating nature of this firearm means that it was intended for a person who might face a number of assailants. Traditionally, they are thought to have been sold to sea captains to face down a mutinous crew, but most duckfoot pistols were actually sold to men who guarded banks or jewelry workshops.

Radiating barrels resemble the foot of a duck

RUPERT OF THE RHINE

In his youth, Prince Rupert of the Rhine (1619–82) was one of the most successful and innovative cavalry commanders in Europe. At the time, conventional cavalry tactics required the men to fire their pistols first to disorganize the enemy formation, and then to charge with the sword. Rupert taught his men to charge home with the sword first, using their pistols only later if the opportunity presented itself. This allowed Rupert's cavalry to charge at top speed, greatly increasing the impact of their charge.

In later life Rupert turned to science, helping found the Royal Society. He was particularly interested in metallurgy, developing a method of heat-treating gun barrels to make them less prone to distortion caused by the heat of repeated firing.

BRITISH CANNON LIGHTER

The flintlock mechanism was used not only for firing pistols and muskets, but also for discharging artillery. A key problem for gunners was that the powerful recoil of a cannon being fired pushed the weapon back several feet, crushing anyone who was in the way. It was therefore necessary for the gunner to stand well clear of the weapon and its wheels when firing. This cannon lighter was made in Britain about 1805. The gunner would have held the handle while placing the end against the cannon's touch hole. When he pulled the ring, the spark fired the cannon.

Elongated trigger

FLINTLOCK CANNON LIGHTER

This cannon lighter dates to around 1780 and was made in Britain. It has a conventional flintlock mechanism operated by a trigger at the far end of the wooden stock. The tip of the tool is encased in brass to minimize the chances of a stray spark being created when it tapped against the iron cannon barrel.

PERSIAN PISTOL

An amazingly ornate pistol made in Persia (now Iran) in the 18th century. Most gold decoration of this date was inlaid or engraved, but in this gun the gold has been cut in filigree fashion from a thin sheet of pure gold and then overlaid onto the weapon.

Gold inlay even extends to flintlock mechanism

BELGIAN PISTOL

This pistol was made in 1810 and seems to have been intended for naval use. It was manufactured in what is now Belgium, but was then a part of France. The area had for centuries been owned by Spain, but was annexed by Revolutionary France in 1794. The weapon was therefore bound for the French navy.

Flintlock mechanism

ADMIRAL NELSON

Admiral Horatio Nelson was born in 1758, and by the time of his death in battle in 1805 had become the greatest naval hero Britain has ever known. Nelson went to sea at the age of 13 and got command of his first ship at the age of 20. As a naval officer, Nelson's prime sidearm was a sword—at first a cutlass and later a magnificent presentation sword of finest steel. Given that most naval battles were conducted at long range by artillery, this was all he needed.

Nonetheless, naval officers were called upon to board enemy ships and fight hand to hand, and on occasion went ashore to take part in land battles. On such occasions Nelson, along with other naval officers, carried a flintlock pistol as well as his sword. This portrait shows him in his full dress admiral's uniform in 1799, wearing just some of the decorations that he had won by this date. His right sleeve is empty, as two years earlier the arm had been amputated after being smashed by a musket ball.

BALKAN DRESS PISTOL

This curiosity dates to the late 17th or early 18th century and was made in the Balkans. Despite appearances, it is not a weapon at all, but an ornate piece of jewelry. During this period, the Balkans were a complex patchwork of semi-independent states divided between the Moslem Ottoman Empire and the Christian Austrian Empire. Control shifted frequently and feuds were common. Custom dictated men go armed at all times, but it was forbidden to carry weapons to meet a ruler for fear of assassination. The answer was for a man to wear a false pistol, such as this, on formal occasions.

Fine scrollwork make it worthy of display before a ruler

PISTOL-SWORD

A few pistols were fitted with bayonets borrowed from muskets, but this is a purpose-built weapon. The sword blade is fixed to the pistol and was the primary weapon. These combination weapons were used mostly by seamen.

Pistol and sword are bolted together

SILESIAN AXE-PISTOL

Silesia, now in Poland but then in Prussia, was a vital center for the iron industry in the 17th century, when this weapon was produced. This weapon takes the form of an axe, with a pistol shooting through the head of the axe. The decorative insets are of bone. The lock plate is, rather unusually, engraved with an elephant—an animal that up to the date of manufacture had never been seen in Silesia.

Elephant engraving

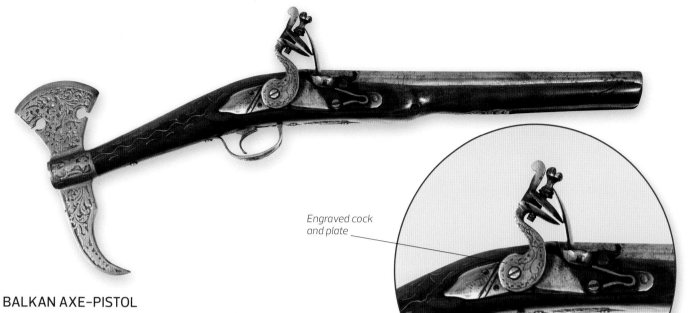

Engraved cock and plate

BALKAN AXE-PISTOL

While the Silesian axe-pistol on page 28 has the axe head at the muzzle, this example from the Balkans has the axe head on the end of the handle. It was made in the 18th century and has inlaid silver wire decoration on the wooden stock. The flintlock is of conventional design, though the cock and plate are engraved, reflecting traditional Balkan taste for decorated weapons.

TINDER LIGHTER

The flintlock was so effective at creating sparks, even in damp conditions, that it was used for purposes other than firing weapons. This example was used to start fires. This example was made in 1820, just six years before English chemist John Walker invented the first match. The lock was loaded with gunpowder, and then placed inside a small pile of wood shavings. When the trigger was pulled, the sparks would set off the gunpowder, which in turn set fire to the shavings.

FRENCH ATELIERS NATIONAUX PISTOL

Made in France about 1790 by Ateliers Nationaux, this pistol is typical of its type. The Ateliers Nationaux were set up by the French government to provide work for the unemployed, setting the men to undertake work useful to the state. This weapon is typically of a very basic pattern and simple design that the semi–skilled laborers could be relied upon to make correctly.

Simple flintlock mechanism

EUROPEAN FLINTLOCK PISTOL

This tiny pistol was designed to fit into a gentleman's coat pocket. The short barrel means it would have been useless at a range of more than a few feet. It was intended to serve as personal protection against footpads or other criminals who would not be able to afford any form of firearm and would be armed with knives.

Opposite side shows brass trim on frame

DOG'S HEAD PISTOL

This small pistol was made in France, probably in the late 18th century. The end of the butt has been carved into the shape of a dog's head. Decorations to the end of the butt were common, as this was the part of the gun that projected from a holster and so would be seen in everyday life.

Walnut and brass dog head design

Grenade or mortar barrel

GRENADE LAUNCHER

Grenades first entered warfare in the Middle Ages, but they did not become common weapons of war until the mid–17th century. At that date they consisted of a thin iron spherical shell filled with gunpowder and detonated by a fuse. These weapons were tried in open battle, but the blast was usually dissipated and they were of little use. When siege warfare became dominant in Europe after about 1650, the grenade came into its own. Thrown into a trench, the blast concentrated by the trench walls would concuss anyone in the area. It became common practice to throw grenades into a trench before assaulting it with musket and bayonet. Throwing a grenade that accurately was difficult, so grenade launchers were invented to improve both the range and accuracy of the grenadiers doing the throwing.

CAUCASIAN MOUNTAINEER'S DRAGON

Although this weapon looks like a flintlock pistol, it is technically a dragon. The dragon was a form of firearm that was popular across Europe from about 1600 to 1700, but then fell out of use. Unlike a conventional pistol, which fired a single lead ball, the dragon fired a number of smaller shot, rather like a modern shotgun. This 18th-century example is from the Caucasian Mountains.

Cock

Shortened cock

Flintlock mechanism

SPANISH FLINTLOCK PISTOL

This elaborate little gun with brass and silver mounts was made in Spain in the 18th century. Its lock is known as the "miquelet," which is a form of the flintlock. The differences between the miquelet and the true flintlock are minor and concern the way the cock is operated by the mainspring and how the trigger releases the mechanism. The miquelet was used most often in the Mediterranean region.

WOODEN FLINTLOCK PISTOL

This highly ornamental pistol was made in Europe in the 17th century. The muzzle end of the barrel is encased in decorative brasswork, while applied pierced metal panels and colored beads decorate the butt and underside of the stock. The decorative work implies that this gun was made for a wealthy customer, while the long barrel indicates it was for use on horseback.

Detail of ornamental brass work

Steel plate

Ramrod

Steel tip to butt

EUROPEAN FLINTLOCK PISTOL

This short weapon is another dragon. The flared muzzle was intended to allow the small balls that it fired to fan out and cover a larger area. This made for a devastating weapon at short range, but a hopelessly inaccurate one at ranges of over 15 feet. Many cavalry regiments in Europe used the name "dragoon" because when they were first raised, they were equipped with these weapons as well as swords.

CANNON-BARRELED PISTOL

This little pistol has what appears to be a military scene of drum and regimental colors crudely engraved onto the lock plate. The quality of the engraving and the crude, flat handle indicates that this was a cheap weapon. The barrel is made to resemble that of a cannon, a feature in fashion in the early 18th century. The lock is unusual in that it sits on top of the barrel, rather than beside it. This meant that the puff of smoke and flame from the lock went upward, not sideways to the right, and may have been an adaptation to a left-handed customer.

Simple etched design on frame

Cannon-shaped barrel

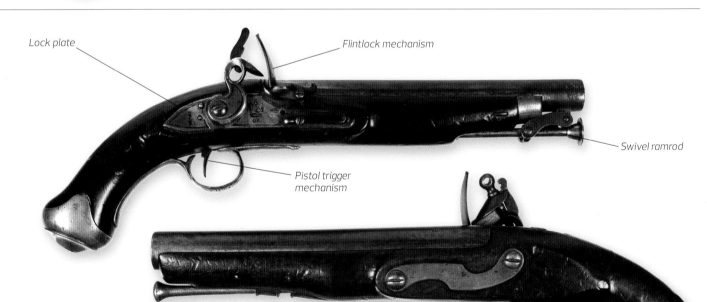

Lock plate

Flintlock mechanism

Pistol trigger mechanism

Swivel ramrod

HENRY NOCK PISTOLS

The celebrated British gunsmith Henry Nock produced a number of different types of guns for the British armed forces in the late 18th century. These pistol feature one of his more successful innovations. The lock and its mechanism are held in place by a number of removable metal pins and screws. The screws are sized so they can be removed using the copper coins that most soldiers could be relied upon to have about their person, thus removing the need for special tools to dismantle and clean the lock.

DUBLIN CASTLE PISTOL

In 1673 Dublin Castle burned down, and the authorities took advantage of the event to demolish the ruins and build a massive complex of government buildings in the heart of the city. Among the new structures put up was a large armaments works where weapons were made for the British army and navy. This pistol was made during the reign of King George III (1738–1820). This example has a caliber of .52 inch with a good quality walnut stock and brass mounts.

Square-shaped bullet

SQUARE-BARRELED FLINTLOCK

The square bullet was an English invention. It was believed that a long slug with a square cross section would turn over when it hit a victim, tearing the flesh and inflicting larger and more damaging wounds. The inventor, one James Puckle, declared that such bullets should be used only against Turks, not against Christians. The slugs were found to be very inaccurate because they tended to tumble in flight and so veered about. This pistol was made in England in the early 18th century.

AMERICAN FLINTLOCK

In 1818 Simeon North of Connecticut invented the very first milling machine to manufacture small metal parts with great precision. This allowed him to manufacture firearms with identical working parts that could be interchanged or replaced immediately without the need to make a new part to order. North made this little pistol five years earlier, when he was still making each part by hand.

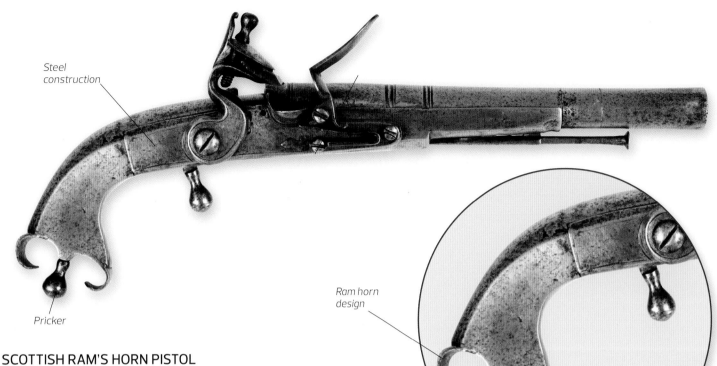

Steel construction

Pricker

Ram horn design

SCOTTISH RAM'S HORN PISTOL

In the 1730s gunsmiths in Doune, near Stirling in Scotland, began producing a distinctive style of pistol that rapidly became popular in the Highlands. By the time this pistol was made in about 1780, the pistols had become part of the regular equipment of British regiments raised in the Highlands. The all-steel design had a strong clip on its left-hand side that fastened on to the cross belt the soldiers wore over their chests. The decorative curls on the butt give this style of weapon its name of "ram's horn" pistol.

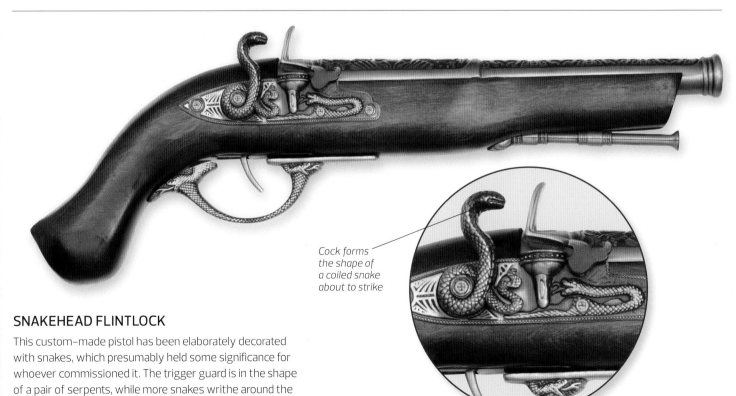

Cock forms the shape of a coiled snake about to strike

SNAKEHEAD FLINTLOCK

This custom-made pistol has been elaborately decorated with snakes, which presumably held some significance for whoever commissioned it. The trigger guard is in the shape of a pair of serpents, while more snakes writhe around the lock plate, and the cock is in the shape of a striking cobra.

DOUBLE-BARRELED PISTOL

This small pistol was made in Europe, probably in the later 18th century. It was designed for personal protection against street robbers. The pan feeds into a cavity in the body of the gun, which drops down to ignite both barrels simultaneously, doubling the stopping power of the pistol.

Double barrels fire at the same time

BRONZE FLINTLOCK

This pistol dates to the 18th century and was made in Europe. The metal fixings are made of bronze, as are the ramrod and the cannon-style barrel. This weapon is highly unusual for its date by having rudimentary sights fitted to the top of the barrel. Most pistols of this date were accurate only at short ranges, so the user just had to point them in the right direction and pull the trigger.

TIPU SULTAN

The Indian ruler Tipu Sultan (1750–99) was an avid collector of pistols, swords and other weapons. Tipu was especially fond of the tiger as a motif, so several of his weapons were decorated with tiger stripes in ebony and gold inlay. Tipu was a cultured ruler of Mysore who introduced important tax and financial reforms to increase the prosperity of his subjects, and the tax take of his government. He is best known, however, as a soldier.

In 1784 he defeated the British in the Second Anglo–Mysore War, forcing them to hand over towns, forts and countryside to him. After defeating other local rulers, Tipu Sultan again faced the British in 1799. This time, the British stormed his capital city of Seringapatem, and Tipu Sultan died gallantly resisting the onslaught. Although it is not known who killed him, a British officer named Arthur Wellesley discovered his body and identified the corpse, feeling the pulse to assure himself that the prince was really dead. Wellesley later went on to become the Duke of Wellington.

PRUSSIAN FLINTLOCK PISTOL

A Prussian army cavalry pistol of the 18th century. This model of pistol was introduced in 1731 and remained in service, with minor changes, until the Napoleonic Wars. The brass band around the muzzle of this example marks it out as being a later model, though its exact date is unknown. The Prussian cavalry were reformed by Frederick the Great during the 1740s and 1750s to become the most feared mounted force in Europe. Their greatest victory was at the Battle of Kesselsdorf in 1745. A massed charge by Prussian cavalry armed with pistols of this style smashed the entire Saxon army, sending it in panicked flight and forcing Saxony to make peace.

SPANISH FLINTLOCK PISTOL

This pistol from Spain has a cannon-style barrel and is highly decorated with chased and pierced metal work. The metal work on the handle is designed to give additional grip in hot weather when the hands of the owner might become sweaty.

Chased and pierced metalwork decoration

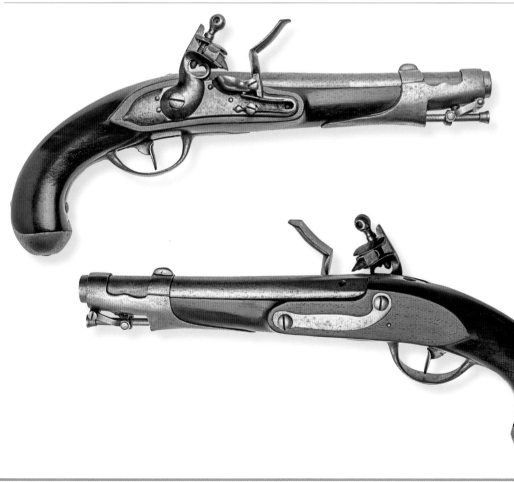

BAVARIAN FLINTLOCK PISTOL

Maximilian III Joseph (1727–77) was the Elector of Bavaria for most of the middle of the 18th century. He inherited a state left prostrate by the War of the Austrian Succession, and was determined to rebuild Bavarian prosperity. He founded the Bavarian Academy of Sciences to encourage learning, reformed the legal code to favor commerce, and patronized innovators in both industry and agriculture. Among the industries that Maximilian encouraged was metalworking, making use of the extensive mineral deposits in Bavaria. These pistols were produced as the Bavarian metal industry began to boom.

Dueling Pistols

Dueling developed during the Renaissance era as a more civilized and fairer alternative to the murderous brawls that young men of the time used to settle differences.

Duels were controlled by strict sets of conventions, which changed over time to suit different cultures and mores. The guiding principle was that the duelists should be given every opportunity to avoid the fight, but that once a fight began it had to be entirely fair.

As a consequence dueling pistols were matching pairs of identical weapons. They were usually loaded by seconds: persons nominated by the duelists to ensure that everything was done properly.

Dueling began to fall out of favor in the later 18th century, when it increasingly began to be seen as a waste of life. By the end of the 19th century it was illegal in most countries.

FRENCH DUELING PISTOLS

These dueling pistols were made in France in the 19th century. The hook on the bottom of the trigger guard allows a finger to be looped around it, giving additional grip and therefore greater accuracy as the trigger is pulled. These examples have twin barrels and so allow each man to fire twice.

Spurred trigger guard

THE BURR–HAMILTON DUEL

The most famous duel in American history took place on July 11, 1804, when the former Secretary of the Treasury Alexander Hamilton and Vice President Aaron Burr faced each other in Weehawken, New Jersey. The dispute began when Dr. Charles Cooper told a newspaper that Hamilton believed Burr to be "a dangerous man, and one who ought not be trusted with the reins of government." Burr demanded an apology, but Hamilton refused to apologize for words spoken by Cooper, not by himself. Burr then asked Hamilton to declare that he did not hold such views. Hamilton refused, so Burr challenged him to a duel. The two met in New Jersey because dueling was illegal in their native New York. Both men fired a single shot. Hamilton missed, but Burr did not. Hamilton was wounded above the right hip and was carried away to Manhattan to be treated, but he died next day. Burr was charged with murder in New York and New Jersey, but fled to South Carolina, before returning to Washington, D.C., to serve out his term as vice president.

BURR–HAMILTON PISTOLS

The Wogdon pistols used during the Burr–Hamilton duel. These English-made pistols were owned by Hamilton's brother-in-law John Baker Church, who lent them to Hamilton for the event. They became controversial immediately after the duel because of their unusual trigger mechanism. The triggers could be set either as normal triggers or as hair triggers. The hair trigger needed much less pressure to fire and so was more accurate, as inadvertent hand movements were less likely. It was alleged that Hamilton had set his own gun to hair trigger, while leaving Burr to use the normal setting—thus giving Hamilton an unfair advantage. Hamilton's second, Nathaniel Pendleton, denied this, saying that he had set both weapons to normal before the duel. The pistols had been used several times before, most notably in the 1801 duel in which Hamilton's son Philip had been killed.

DUELING PISTOLS

When dueling first began, the vast majority of fights were conducted with swords—usually whatever swords the men had to hand. By the middle of the 18th century, however, the British were using pistols more often than swords, and their lead was followed first by the Americans, then by the French. It was felt that pistols were fairer because they gave less of an advantage to an experienced military man than did swords. As pistols became more popular, conventions about their use developed. Either the principals would stand back to back, take an agreed number of paces and then turn and fire, or they would stand an agreed distance apart and fire when one of the seconds gave a signal. Alternatively, the participants might take it in turn to shoot, the man challenged shooting first.

In 1780 Governor General of India Warren Hastings declared that Philip Francis was "devoid of truth and honour." Francis demanded an apology, but Hastings refused. A duel followed. Francis was injured, but recovered.

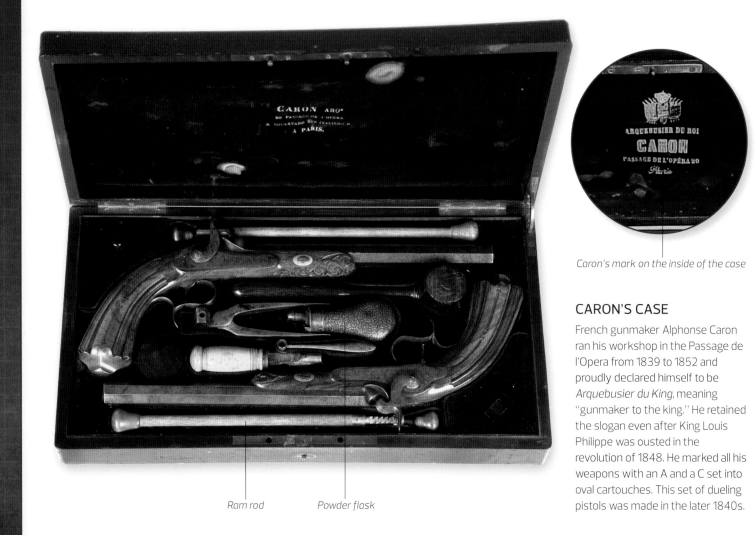

Caron's mark on the inside of the case

Ram rod *Powder flask*

CARON'S CASE

French gunmaker Alphonse Caron ran his workshop in the Passage de l'Opera from 1839 to 1852 and proudly declared himself to be *Arquebusier du King*, meaning "gunmaker to the king." He retained the slogan even after King Louis Philippe was ousted in the revolution of 1848. He marked all his weapons with an A and a C set into oval cartouches. This set of dueling pistols was made in the later 1840s.

GILDED DUELING PISTOLS

A set of ornate French dueling pistols from the second half of the 19th century, embellished with gilding, showing a strangely domestic scene. In this set, the precautions taken to ensure that neither man had an advantage have been taken to an extreme. Not only are there the standard powder flask, cleaning rods and other accessories all mounted in a wooden case, there is even a small crucible in which lead can be melted and molds for the molten metal to be turned into bullets. This way the seconds could ensure that even the bullets were identical.

Gilding adds an even more elegant touch to the engraving that decorates these pistols.

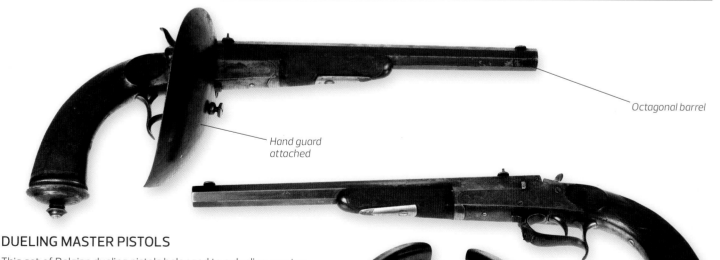

Octagonal barrel

Hand guard attached

DUELING MASTER PISTOLS

This set of Belgian dueling pistols belonged to a dueling master. These masters were usually retired soldiers who taught young men how to fight with pistol or sword in preparation for the day they might join the army or fight a duel. When practicing a duel with pistols, the men fired wax bullets at each other, enabling them to see if they hit or missed an opponent without causing serious injury. The curious metal shields were designed to fit in front of the trigger guard and are a training device to protect bare hands.

Distinctive hand guard

ACCURACY AND RELIABILITY

Most pistol duels were fought at a distance of about 40 or 50 feet. Given the inaccuracy of flintlock pistols in the 18th century this was not as deadly as it may sound. Duels might be for one shot each, an agreed number of shots or until one or the other participant was hit. It gradually came to be accepted that honor had been satisfied so long as both men turned up ready and prepared to fight. Once this had been done, the seconds very often managed to sort out a form of apology that would remove the need for any shots to be fired. Alternatively, one of the participants might deliberately fire his shot into the ground at his feet, after which it was considered appropriate for the other to do likewise. A man who broke the conventions could find himself arrested for murder or ostracized by his friends and family.

An illustration of the duel between Eugene Onegin and Vladimir Lensky, from the verse novel Eugene Onegin *by Alexander Pushkin*

Scallop motif

Finely carved grip

BELGIAN DUELING PISTOLS

This fine pair of dueling pistols was made in Belgium during the middle of the 19th century. By this date dueling was the preserve of young, wealthy, aristocratic men, and so the weapons were usually of high quality and price. This pair uses the percussion–cap system, which was more reliable than the flintlock and so made dueling a considerably more dangerous activity than before.

TWIGG DUELING PISTOLS

John Twigg, a famous gunsmith who operated his business in London's fashionable Piccadilly Street from 1776 to 1795, made this pair of pistols. He produced high-class firearms himself, but also employed a host of craftsmen to mass-produce cheaper weapons to his design. This particular pair has been considerably altered. In the 19th century, they were converted from flintlock to the new percussion-cap system, and at some point have had spring-loaded bayonets added.

Incised checkering on butt

Octagonal barrel

ENGLISH DUELING PISTOLS

Benjamin Griffin and his son Joseph made guns in London from 1724 to 1770. They specialized in high-quality guns, made specifically to order by aristocratic clients. The guns often featured silver or silver-gilt mounts, chasing and other details. This pair of pistols is described as a pair of dueling pistols, though their short barrels would seem to indicate that they are personal protection weapons.

WELLINGTON VERSUS WINCHILSEA

In 1829 the British prime minister—and victor at the Battle of Waterloo—was steering legislation through Parliament to free Catholics from centuries-old legislation restricting their civil rights. The Earl of Winchilsea accused him of "an insidious design for the infringement of our liberties and the introduction of Popery into every department of the State." Wellington challenged the earl to a duel. The two met on March 21 at Battersea. When the signal was given to fire, Winchilsea kept his arm by his side, pistol pointing down. Seeing this, Wellington fired wide. Lord Winchilsea then apologized for his words.

Percussion Weapons

Flintlock weapons were relatively easy to make and to use. The business of loading, however, was complicated and time consuming. Moreover, the fact that loose gunpowder had to be sprinkled into the pan before the pan cover was brought down meant that it was virtually impossible to fire a flintlock in the rain, and even in mist they were liable to misfire. Yet for generations there seemed to be no alternative. Gunsmiths could refine the action, add a smoother operating mechanism and generally produce a better gun, but the basic deficiencies of the flintlock remained. It was not until technology advanced that a replacement was made.

EARLY-AMERICAN PERCUSSION PISTOL

This early American percussion-cap pistol is a smoothbore, single-shot weapon. The gun is loaded from the muzzle, then the percussion cap fitted on to the nipple and the hammer pulled back, ready to be fired.

Percussion cap

Nipple

Cap fits over nipple

PERCUSSION BREECHLOCK PISTOL

Made in Europe about 1850, this small pistol has a pivoting breech-loading system. To load the pistol the breech is lifted, as shown here. The charge, bullet and wadding are then pushed into the breech, which is then lowered back so that it is flush to the barrel. The percussion cap is then put on the nipple and the gun is ready to fire.

THE PERCUSSION CAP

The percussion cap was a revolution in firearms design, but it was slow to develop. It was in 1800 that British scientist Edward Howard invented fulminates that would explode or catch fire when hit hard enough—previous explosives had needed a spark or flame to set them off. Seven years later a Scottish vicar named Alexander Forsyth came up with the idea of using fulminates to fire a gun. He removed the flint from his flintlock, replacing it with a hammer, and put fulminates in the pan in place of gunpowder. When the hammer struck the pan it set off the fulminates, which then fired the gun in the normal way.

The next step seems to have been invented independently by a number of men between 1817 and 1820, including American Joshua Shaw, Frenchman François Prélat and Englishman Peter Hawker. This involved removing the pan and replacing it with a hollow tube—called the "nipple"—that led from the breech

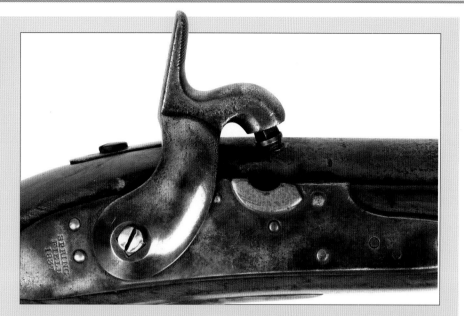

end of the barrel to where the pan would have been. The fulminate was no longer scattered on the pan, but instead fitted inside a thin metal cup. This was placed over the nipple, so that the fulminate faced down the tube inside the nipple. What had been the cock in a flintlock holding the flint now became a hammer. There was usually a spike or flange sticking up from the back of the hammer so that it could be

pulled back with the thumb into the cocked position. When the trigger was pulled the hammer was flung forward by the spring to strike the back of the cap. The blow slammed the cap against the nipple, creating an impact that set off the fulminate. The explosion pushed super-heated gasses down the tube inside the nipple to detonate the main charge of gunpowder inside the barrel and fire the gun.

Hammer rather than cock-and-flint

Brass barrel

SPANISH PISTOL

The earliest percussion systems were not always reliable. This short Spanish pistol combines both Forsyth primer and percussion-cap mechanisms in one weapon. The lock pan uses both the early Forsyth system and the later percussion cap.

Flintlock to Percussion System Conversions

The advantages of the percussion system were obvious to all, and many people wanted to get their hands on a percussion-cap gun as quickly as possible. Buying an entirely new gun, however, was a costly business, so many people chose instead to convert their existing flintlock gun to a percussion-cap gun. The amount of adaptation needed was not great. The barrel remained the same, as did the ammunition and gunpowder charge. It was only the hammer and nipple that needed to be acquired to replace the cock and pan.

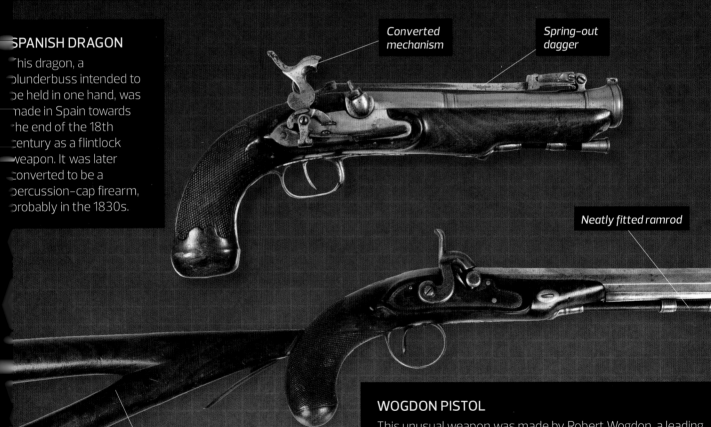

SPANISH DRAGON

This dragon, a blunderbuss intended to be held in one hand, was made in Spain towards the end of the 18th century as a flintlock weapon. It was later converted to be a percussion-cap firearm, probably in the 1830s.

Converted mechanism

Spring-out dagger

Neatly fitted ramrod

Wooden shoulder stock

WOGDON PISTOL

This unusual weapon was made by Robert Wogdon, a leading London gunsmith active from the 1760s until his retirement in 1803. The detachable wooden stock was designed to turn this long pistol into a short carbine that could be fired from the shoulder for added accuracy and stability. This sort of high-quality weapon would have been expensive to replace, so the conversion to percussion cap was a natural move.

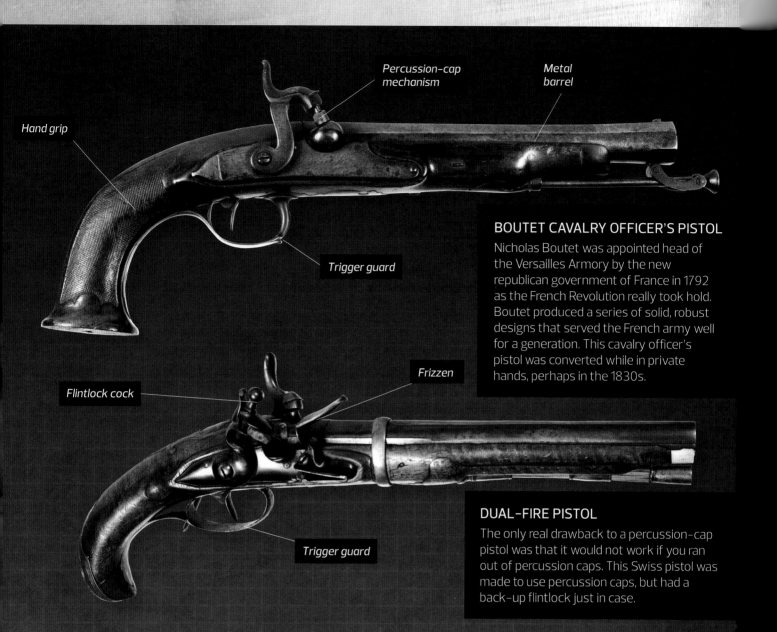

Percussion-cap mechanism

Metal barrel

Hand grip

Trigger guard

BOUTET CAVALRY OFFICER'S PISTOL

Nicholas Boutet was appointed head of the Versailles Armory by the new republican government of France in 1792 as the French Revolution really took hold. Boutet produced a series of solid, robust designs that served the French army well for a generation. This cavalry officer's pistol was converted while in private hands, perhaps in the 1830s.

Frizzen

Flintlock cock

Trigger guard

DUAL-FIRE PISTOL

The only real drawback to a percussion-cap pistol was that it would not work if you ran out of percussion caps. This Swiss pistol was made to use percussion caps, but had a back-up flintlock just in case.

NAPOLEON III OF FRANCE

When the Emperor Napoleon died in 1821 he left a son, who died in 1832. The prestige of the imperial cause and the liberal policies it espoused were inherited by Napoleon's nephew Louis Napoleon. The dashing young Louis Napoleon joined the Swiss army and earned a reputation as a competent officer and left-wing firebrand. In 1840, spurred on by reports of unrest in France, Louis Napoleon moved to England where he recruited a small force of supporters and bought enough percussion-cap weapons to arm them. On August 6, the little army landed at Boulogne. Louis Napoleon strode ashore calling on all loyal Frenchman to join him. He was at once arrested, disarmed and thrown into prison. Eight years later he tried the ballot box, got himself elected president of France and then declared himself emperor of France.

LONG-BARRELED PISTOLS

Pistols with unusually long barrels have been produced in small numbers from the moment the pistol was invented right to the present day. The main purpose of such a barrel has usually been to improve accuracy, without a person being required to purchase a carbine or rifle. In the days of smoothbore muzzle loaders, accuracy was heavily dependent on the length of a barrel, as the longer barrel would reduce the amount of movement adopted by the ball as it left the gun (most balls in those days being slightly smaller than the bore of the barrel to make loading easier). Once rifling had become common, length was no longer so crucial; however, target-shooting pistols would often have a longer barrel to increase the distance between the rear sight and the foresight. This gave the shooter greater precision of aiming when using normal open metal sights.

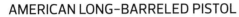

AMERICAN LONG-BARRELED PISTOL

J. Stevens Arms made this long-barreled pistol in the late 19th century. Joshua Stevens founded his company in 1864 to produce target pistols as well as smaller-caliber shotguns and rifles. This elegant percussion-cap pistol is typical of the company's output at this date. In 1920 the company was bought by Savage Arms and now produces low-cost weapons of various designs.

LONG-BARRELED PERCUSSION PISTOL

This distinctive percussion-cap pistol was made in France in about 1850. The spur on the trigger guard allows the finger to curl around it to provide extra grip. The unusual feature of this gun is that the barrel comes in two parts and can be unscrewed. The additional six inches of barrel included a foresight for target shooting, while the shorter barrel had no such sight and may have been used for dueling.

Steadying spur

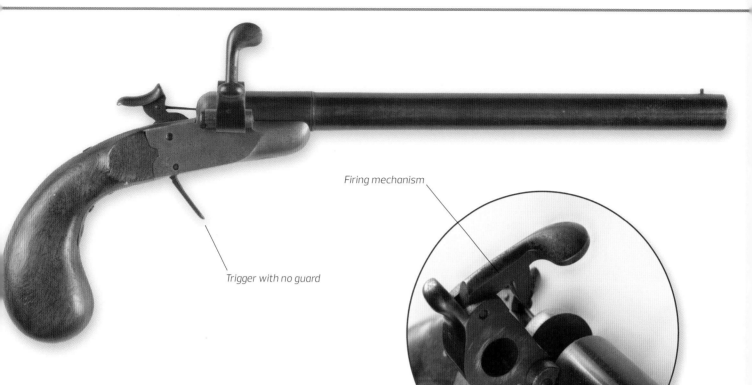

Firing mechanism

Trigger with no guard

LORON SINGLE-SHOT PISTOL

Made in 1835 by Loron in France, this single-shot pistol uses the needle-gun system. The paper cartridge was loaded from the breech end. Inside the cartridge was a percussion cap, gunpowder and bullet. When the trigger was pulled, the hammer drove a needle into the cartridge, striking the cap and detonating the powder.

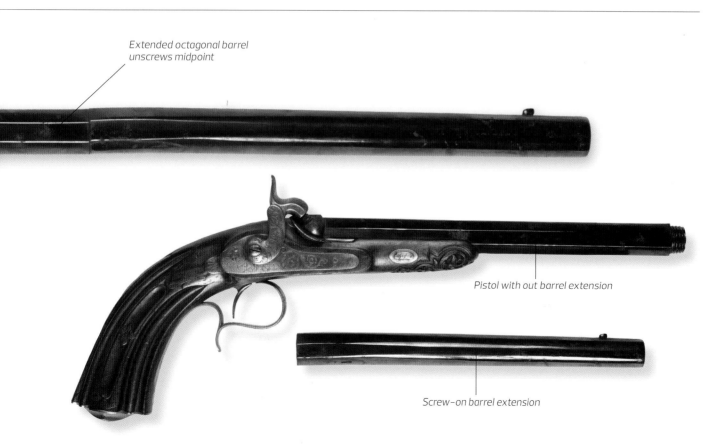

Extended octagonal barrel
unscrews midpoint

Pistol with out barrel extension

Screw-on barrel extension

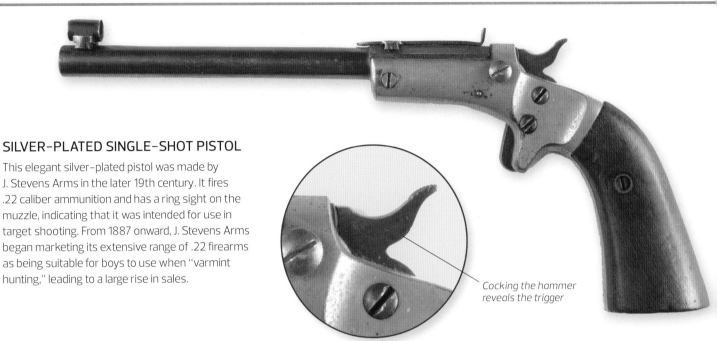

SILVER-PLATED SINGLE-SHOT PISTOL

This elegant silver-plated pistol was made by J. Stevens Arms in the later 19th century. It fires .22 caliber ammunition and has a ring sight on the muzzle, indicating that it was intended for use in target shooting. From 1887 onward, J. Stevens Arms began marketing its extensive range of .22 firearms as being suitable for boys to use when "varmint hunting," leading to a large rise in sales.

Cocking the hammer reveals the trigger

Double triggers

BELGIAN DOUBLE-BARRELED PISTOL

This small doubled-barreled pistol from 19th-century Belgium has a clever design that enables it to fire without an external hammer. When the trigger is pushed forward, the barrel flips down to allow cartridges to be loaded, while at the same time cocking the internal hammer. When the barrel is closed and clicks into place, it is ready to be fired by pulling the trigger back. There are two triggers, one for each barrel.

Pistol in loading position

Decorative grip

Triggers

BELGIAN DOUBLE-BARRELED PISTOL

This Belgian pistol loads like a modern shotgun, the barrels hinging down to allow cartridges to be inserted from the breech. The mechanism is otherwise a fairly conventional percussion-cap action.

Opposite side of the barrel showing etched metal design

VERY GUN

A gun designed to fire flares into the air as a signaling device was first invented by American naval officer Edward Very in the 1870s. As a consequence, all such guns are commonly termed "very guns" and the flares they fire "very lights," even when, as with this 19th-century British example, it was not designed by Very himself.

Pistol in loading position

ENGLISH LANCASTER PISTOL

The Lancaster was a mid-to-late-19th-century British pistol that had four barrels, usually chambered to take .450 centerfire cartridges, though other models with similarly heavy lead bullets were available. The pistol was marketed to army officers serving in colonial areas where battles against spear-armed enemies who rushed out of cover had shown the need for a weapon that had a high rate of fire and great stopping power.

DARRA PISTOL

This single-shot, breech-loading pistol was made in the 19th century in the Indian town of Darra Adam Khel, now in Pakistan. It is chambered to fire 12-gauge shotgun cartridges and is therefore more properly called a dragon. The town still produces weapons, from pistols to anti-aircraft guns, in a large number of small workshops.

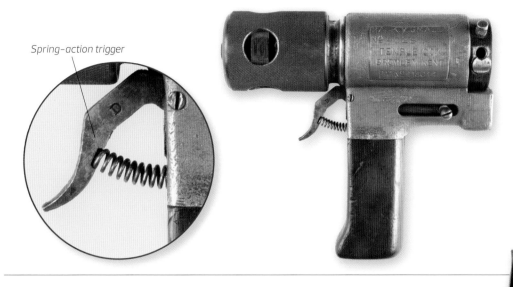

Spring-action trigger

TEMPLE COX HUMANE ANIMAL KILLER

This small weapon is a humane killer made by Temple Cox. A .22 caliber blank is inserted at the rear, and the breech closed. When fired, the blank fires a bolt several inches forward, the bolt then being retracted by a spring. When placed flush against the skull of the animal to be slaughtered, the bolt punches a fatal wound into the skull.

BRITISH PERCUSSION REVOLVER

Equipped with a handle of polished walnut wood, this single-shot percussion-cap pistol was made in Britain in the mid-19th century. The barrel and case are, unusually, made of cast bronze.

FOUR-BARRELED DERRINGER-STYLE PISTOL

This peculiar little pocket pistol has four barrels, each of which was loaded independently from the barrel. On the underside are four hammers and percussion nipples, one for each barrel. When the trigger is pulled it successively fires each barrel.

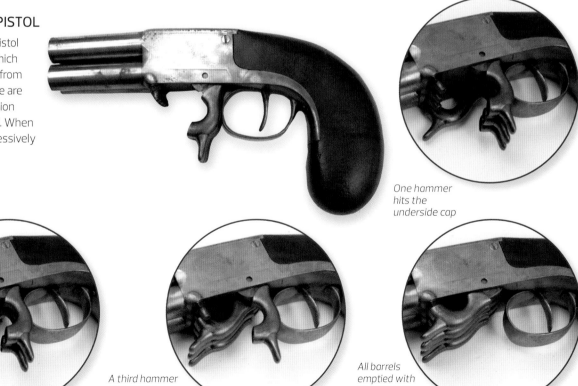

One hammer hits the underside cap

Two hammers engaged, two primed to go

A third hammer struck and third barrel fires

All barrels emptied with all hammers engaged

Repeating Weapons

The Industrial Revolution

The craftsmen who individually made firearms from the 14th to the 19th centuries were highly skilled designers and manufacturers. Some of the weapons they produced were superlative for their time, but all gunmakers were restricted by the materials they worked with and the lack of standardization inherent in the crafting process. During the course of the 19th century, the Industrial Revolution revolutionized gun design and production. New explosives, new metal alloys and new manufacturing techniques all came together to make new and deadlier forms of firearms.

THE PURSUIT. Repeating handguns came into their own in the mid-19th century. In America, Colt five-shooters provided Texas Rangers with a crucial advantage against the Comanches during the Texas–Indian Wars (1820–1875). They could aim, fire and reload the revolvers while in pursuit of the enemy. That success led the U.S. government to contract Colt to produce a six-shot version for troops fighting the Mexican–American War (1846–1848).

Pepperboxes and Derringers

Around 1790, British gunsmiths perfected what had until then been a rarely used concept with little success, producing the pepperbox pistol. These weapons had only one firing mechanism but multiple barrels. The barrels were arranged in a cylinder that could rotate around a central hub. As each barrel was fired, the user turned the cylinder to bring a new barrel into line with the firing mechanism.

The name—believed to have been coined by the writer Mark Twain—comes from the gun's similarity to a domestic pepper grinder. The flintlock firing mechanism meant that stray sparks might set off extra barrels unless the weapon was kept scrupulously clean, so the pepperbox became very popular after the percussion cap was introduced and solved the problem.

About the same time that percussion caps were developed, a new self-cocking mechanism was introduced. This meant that the cylinder no longer needed to be rotated by hand. As the trigger was pulled, a lever moved the cylinder on and pulled back the hammer ready to fire. Ethan Allen of Massachusetts, who patented it in 1837, perfected this system in the United States. The weapon acquired an enviable reputation and was sold in large numbers to Easterners heading out west to take part in the California Gold Rush of the 1840s.

Not long after the introduction of pepperboxes, Henry Deringer inherited a gunsmith business from his father and began producing guns in Philadelphia in 1806. At first he worked on government contracts, producing rifles for both the army and for trade with indigenous tribes. In 1825, however, he produced the weapon that would make his fortune and be forever linked to his name.

Small, personal-defense weapons of the time tended to be small-caliber weapons, making them easy to carry in pockets. These lacked the stopping power needed to knock down an assailant. Deringer produced a pocket pistol that was robustly built so that it could cope with a heavy charge of powder and with a wide bore so that it could fire a heavy lead slug. Within a year he was selling every gun he could make. Other companies copied the idea, calling their weapons "derringers" (with a double "r") to avoid copyright issues.

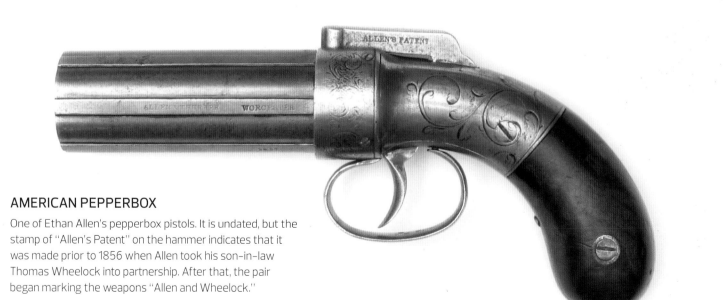

AMERICAN PEPPERBOX

One of Ethan Allen's pepperbox pistols. It is undated, but the stamp of "Allen's Patent" on the hammer indicates that it was made prior to 1856 when Allen took his son-in-law Thomas Wheelock into partnership. After that, the pair began marking the weapons "Allen and Wheelock."

Floral scroll engraved frame

Ring trigger

Barrels show the distinctive wavy pattern of Damascus steel

MARIETTE BREVETÉ PISTOL

A finely made pistol produced in Belgium by Guillaume Mariette, who ran a small factory at Liege from 1832 to 1865. This particular pepperbox has four removable barrels of Damascus steel and an elaborately engraved frame. Unlike weapons made in Britain or America, this pepperbox fires the bottom barrel when the trigger is pulled.

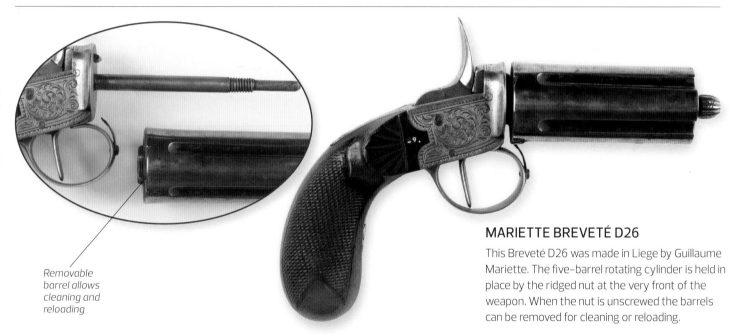

Removable barrel allows cleaning and reloading

MARIETTE BREVETÉ D26

This Breveté D26 was made in Liege by Guillaume Mariette. The five-barrel rotating cylinder is held in place by the ridged nut at the very front of the weapon. When the nut is unscrewed the barrels can be removed for cleaning or reloading.

HOWDAH PISTOL

British colonial officials in India found that they had a need for a powerful handgun when out in more remote areas, where they might unexpectedly encounter tigers, bears and other large aggressive animals at close range. At first the officials carried old rifles, cut down to a fraction of their length, but then sent back to Britain for weapons made specifically for this purpose. The result was the so-called howdah pistol, which took its name from the howdah—a carriage in which people rode on the back of elephants. The weapons were typically short, with a wide bore and robustly built to take a powerful charge of powder. This unmarked percussion-cap howdah pistol has two barrels.

ENGLISH PEPPERBOX

This small pepperbox was made in England about 1850, but does not carry a maker's mark to allow it to be dated more precisely. Its small size indicates that it was intended to be carried in a coat pocket.

Classic deep-cut scrollwork decorates the frame

NORTH & COUCH GAMESHOOTER

Unlike most pepperbox pistols, this peculiar little weapon made in the United States in the 1860s was designed to fire all its barrels at the same time. It was marketed as a pistol to be whipped out and fired at small game when the opportunity presented, hence its name.

ALLEN & THURBER PEPPERBOX

This pepperbox pistol is marked Allen and Thurber, indicating that famous gunsmith Ethan Allen made it to a design patented by Thurber. The nipples and percussion caps at the rear of the barrels are masked by a nipple shield that stopped the caps from falling off. This model has six barrels and fires .36 caliber balls.

FRENCH PEPPERBOX

This small French pepperbox pistol has a silver-plated body with gold inlay, though much of this has worn off since the weapon was made in around 1840. Its small size indicates that it was intended for personal protection, while its high quality shows it was aimed at the gentry.

Scrollwork engraving forming a nautilus shape on the frame

TURNOVER PISTOL

This unmarked British percussion-cap pistol probably dates to around 1840. The four barrels rotate, but this is not a true pepperbox. Termed a turnover pistol, the two triggers operate the twin hammers to fire the upper barrels. Once they have been discharged, the barrels are rotated and new percussion caps put on the nipples to fire the remaining two barrels.

Four individual barrels

Harmonica-style barrel

THREE-SHOT PISTOL

This unusual little weapon belongs to a class known as "harmonica pistols," as the barrels are constructed side-by-side and drilled from a single block of metal. The precise date of this unmarked weapon is unknown, but it probably comes from central Europe and may date to the 1860s.

THOMAS LLOYD TURNOVER PISTOLS

This pair of tiny percussion-cap pistols was made by gunsmith Thomas Lloyd in London. They are of the turnover variety, as the barrels rotate to be fired by the sole percussion mechanism.

THE DERRINGER

Although intended for personal protection against assailants, the derringer was widely used in other circumstances. Gamblers in the American West famously carried derringers in their vest pockets so that they could appear to be nonthreatening and yet still produce a weapon if accused of cheating. It became normal for a professional gambler to start the day by firing his derringer into the ground and then reloading it with a fresh charge that could be relied upon to work. More ominously, the derringer acquired a reputation, at least in fiction, of being the favored weapon of evil women intent on murder. The most famous real-life use of a derringer came on April 14, 1865, when

well-known actor John Wilkes Booth used a rifled derringer pistol to shoot U.S. President Abraham Lincoln in the back of the head at point-blank range. Lincoln died within hours.

LADY'S CASE WITH PISTOL COMPARTMENT

Among the companies that copied the original Deringer format to market rival "derringers" was Colt. The prestige of the Colt name ensured them a ready export market that Deringer could not achieve. This pair of Model No. 3 Derringers was made in the final quarter of the 19th century and exported to England. There, Halstaffe of Regent Street incorporated them into this lady's traveling makeup box. The upper parts of the case hold perfume, tweezers and other vanity items, while the pistols are in the lower drawer.

Lady's vanity case

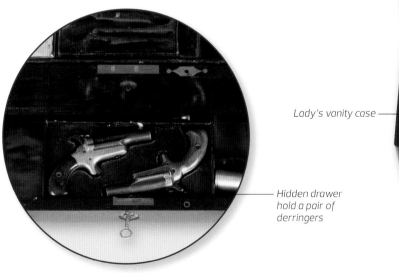

Hidden drawer hold a pair of derringers

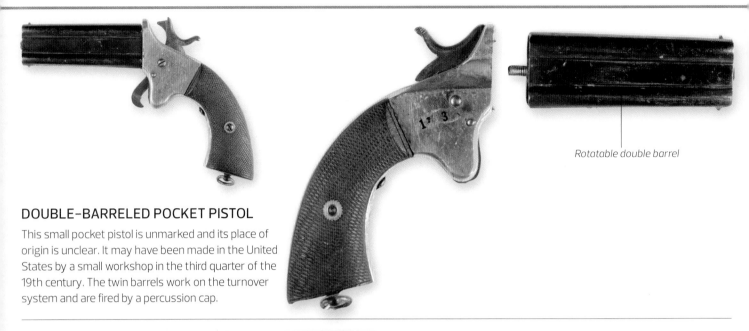

DOUBLE-BARRELED POCKET PISTOL

This small pocket pistol is unmarked and its place of origin is unclear. It may have been made in the United States by a small workshop in the third quarter of the 19th century. The twin barrels work on the turnover system and are fired by a percussion cap.

Rotatable double barrel

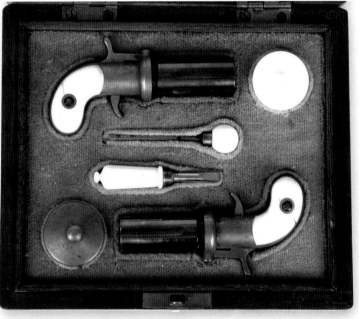

ENGLISH MINIATURE PISTOLS

The barrels of these two pistols are just one inch long, and the caliber of the barrel is less than a 10th of an inch. They are expertly made by London gunsmith John Maycock. Each pistol has an ivory handle, brass body and blued-steel twin barrels. The barrels are of the foldover variety: once one barrel has been fired, the other can be turned to come up to the percussion-cap mechanism to be fired. Maycock specialized in making very small pistols, neatly packed into wooden boxes along with accessories such as a powder flask, screwdriver, cleaning rod and lubricating oil. Even today, his weapons are much sought after by collectors and command high prices.

BOXLOCK PISTOL

This tiny three-inch-long pistol is unmarked and has lost its original wooden box, but it most likely dates to the early or mid-19th century. The barrel and body are made of brass, while the tiny powder flask is of copper. This kind of pistol is called a "boxlock" because all the working mechanisms for the hammer and the trigger are located in a "box" or receiver directly below the top-mounted hammer.

Octagonal barrel

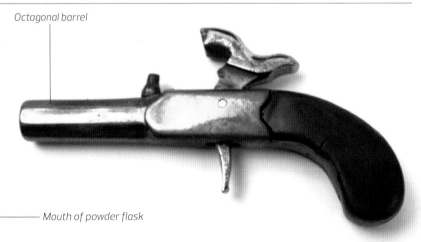

Mouth of powder flask

PINFIRE PEPPERBOX

This cast-iron pepperbox was made in France in the mid-19th century. It is made to fire paper cartridges with an internal percussion cap by the pinfire method. In this firing method, the priming compound is ignited by striking a small pin which protrudes radially from just above the base of the cartridge.

The metal loop attached to the trigger is just large enough to go around the wrist and was presumably intended to stop the weapon being dropped in a brawl.

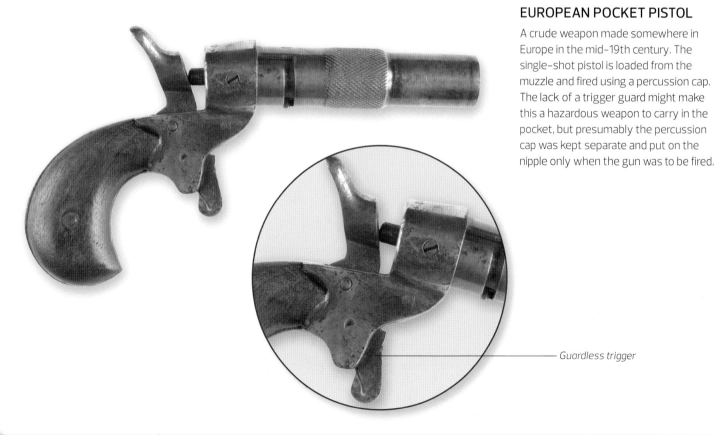

Wrist loop

EUROPEAN POCKET PISTOL

A crude weapon made somewhere in Europe in the mid-19th century. The single-shot pistol is loaded from the muzzle and fired using a percussion cap. The lack of a trigger guard might make this a hazardous weapon to carry in the pocket, but presumably the percussion cap was kept separate and put on the nipple only when the gun was to be fired.

Guardless trigger

PERCUSSION-CAP PISTOL

A small, simple yet well-made single-shot pistol from the mid-19th century. The octagonal barrel is mounted on a small body and is some two inches in length.

Round steel barrels

Broad-leaf floral scroll and punch-dot design embellishes nickel plating.

Two-piece rosewood grips

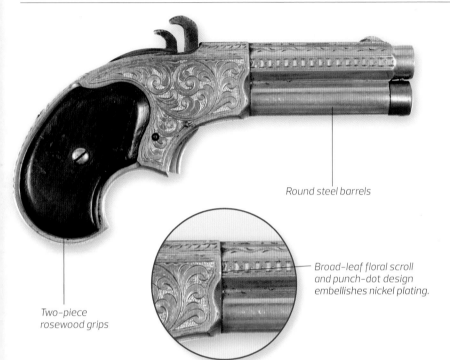

REMINGTON RIDER MAGAZINE PISTOL

This elegant little weapon was made by Remington Arms, a company founded in Ilion, New York, in 1816 to make rifle barrels by blacksmith Eliphalet Remington. The business thrived, and soon Remington was making a wide variety of firearms and ammunition.

This Remington Rider pistol is unusual in that it has a magazine holding five rounds of .32 cartridges in the tube beneath the barrel. When the two hammers were pulled back, they operated a mechanism that ejected the spent cartridge. As the larger hammer was pushed back, it pulled a new cartridge into position, while the smaller hammer remained back until the gun was fired.

Sideways-mounted hammer

Seven-shot cylinder designed side-on to the gun

TURRET GUN

John Webster Cochrane of New York was an innovative gunsmith who patented a large number of weapon designs, not all of them successful. This turret gun was one of his least successful, as only five are known to have been made. The seven cartridges were placed into the round disk, the "turret" of the name, which was then mounted onto the spindle. The hammer is the bar running across the front of the turret. As each shot was fired, the turret turned to bring the next cartridge in line with the barrel.

Samuel Colt

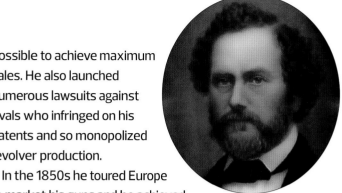

America's most famous gunsmith, Samuel Colt was born in Hartford, Connecticut, in 1814. After a spell at sea, Colt went to work at his father's textile business in 1832. He then began working on an idea for a gun that had a single barrel, but a revolving chamber of cartridges that came into line with the barrel in turn. Other similar designs had been seen before, but Colt's breakthrough was his perfection of a pawl that locked the rotating cylinder exactly in place with great precision.

In 1847 the Texas Rangers placed an order for 1,000 of these new revolvers, giving Colt enough money to establish his own factory. Always a businessman as much an inventor, Colt deliberately priced his gun as low as possible to achieve maximum sales. He also launched numerous lawsuits against rivals who infringed on his patents and so monopolized revolver production.

In the 1850s he toured Europe to market his guns and he achieved massive sales. Late in life Colt encountered controversy when he sold guns to both sides in the American Civil War, though he failed to see what the fuss was about. He died of gout in 1862, leaving $15 million (then an enormous sum of money) to his wife and children.

Five-chambered barrel

TEXAS PATERSON REVOLVER

The Texas Paterson was Colt's first commercially produced revolver. It was patented in 1836 and lacks some of the refinements Colt added later. The revolving cylinder contains five chambers, each of which has to be loaded separately with gunpowder and lead ball. The only way to do this is to remove the cylinder from the pistol, though it was possible to have spare cylinders that could be loaded and kept in a pocket. Percussion caps were placed on the nipples at the rear of the cylinder.

Simple mass-produced interchangeable parts

Exposed chamber for a percussive revolver showing exposed "nipples" onto which percussion caps would be placed

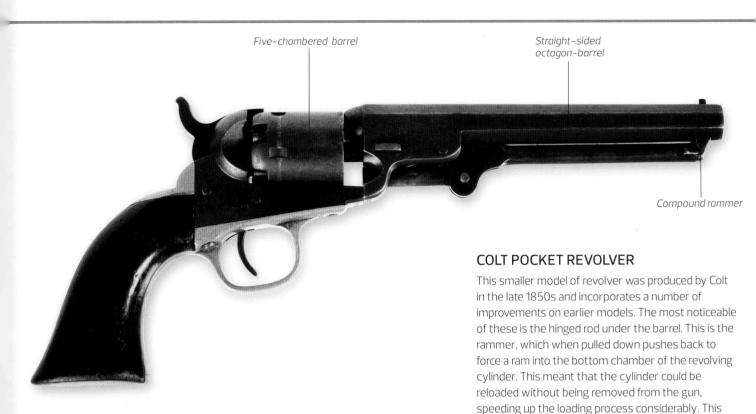

Five-chambered barrel

Straight-sided octagon-barrel

Compound rammer

COLT POCKET REVOLVER

This smaller model of revolver was produced by Colt in the late 1850s and incorporates a number of improvements on earlier models. The most noticeable of these is the hinged rod under the barrel. This is the rammer, which when pulled down pushes back to force a ram into the bottom chamber of the revolving cylinder. This meant that the cylinder could be reloaded without being removed from the gun, speeding up the loading process considerably. This example belonged to a Unionist officer killed at the Second Battle of Bull Run (Manassas) in 1862.

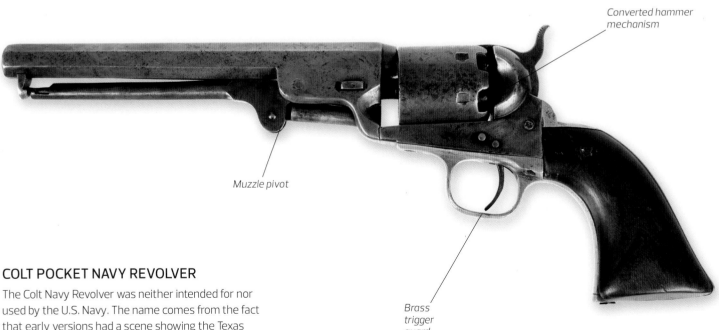

Converted hammer mechanism

Muzzle pivot

Brass trigger guard

COLT POCKET NAVY REVOLVER

The Colt Navy Revolver was neither intended for nor used by the U.S. Navy. The name comes from the fact that early versions had a scene showing the Texas navy's victory at the Battle of Campeche engraved on the cylinder. This was a marketing ploy to back up Colt's claim that the Texan officers had carried his pistols during the battle. The pistol fired .36 balls and, unlike earlier Colt revolvers, was small enough to carry in a belt holster. This is the "pocket" version, which has a shorter barrel.

COLT'S MANUFACTURING COMPANY

Samuel Colt founded his first firearms company in 1836 with the distinctly uncatchy title of "Patent Arms Manufacturing Company of Paterson, New Jersey, Colt's Patent." The company's products proved to be as uninspiring as its name. Although the Colt Paterson was an ingenious and impressive weapon, manufacturing quality was poor. Those sold to the U.S. Army were particularly variable in quality, and by 1842 the company had stopped manufacturing completely. For the next six years Colt designs were made by the Whitney Armory, with Colt taking a $10 royalty on every weapon sold.

By 1848 Colt had saved up enough money to try manufacturing again. This time he founded Colt's Patent Firearms Manufacturing Company in

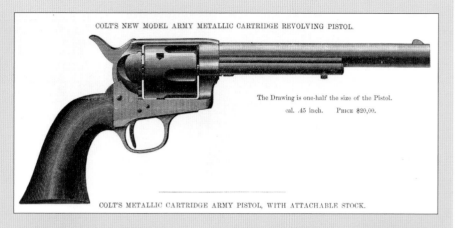

COLT'S NEW MODEL ARMY METALLIC CARTRIDGE REVOLVING PISTOL.

The Drawing is one-half the size of the Pistol.
cal. .45 inch.   PRICE $20.00.

COLT'S METALLIC CARTRIDGE ARMY PISTOL, WITH ATTACHABLE STOCK.

The original Colt Armory was built in 1855 in the district of Hartford known as Coltsville. It was destroyed by fire in 1864, and rebuilt with its most dramatic feature of the original structure, the blue onion dome with gold stars, topped by a gold orb and a rampant colt, the original symbol of Colt's Manufacturing Company.

Hartford, Connecticut, and built a factory beside the Connecticut River. The business did well, largely due to new working practices introduced by Colt.

Colt set himself up as a model employer determined to have a contented and productive workforce. All workers were given an hour for lunch, and the working day was restricted to 10 hours—then considered short. There was a clubhouse adjacent to the factory where workers had access to a library, newspapers and games. Next to his factory, Colt built a development of good-quality homes that his workers could rent for relatively low sums on a weekly or monthly basis. In return, Colt expected top-quality work and hard labor from his workers. He would routinely dismiss on the spot anyone who turned up late or who produced below-standard products.

The new idea of standardized, interchangeable parts was taken up with enthusiasm by Colt. Instead of each pistol being made from scratch, he developed an early form of the assembly line. Each component of the gun was mass-produced to be identical, and then the gun was assembled from the various interchangeable components. This enabled him to reduce production costs by reducing the need for skilled labor in the workforce.

Colt set out to be an aggressive salesman and publicist for his weapons. In 1851, at the London Exhibition, he took apart 10 revolvers, mixed up all the parts and put 10 revolvers back together, which all worked perfectly. This convinced the British of the practice of interchangeability, and the Royal Navy placed an order for 4,000 revolvers. Colt opened a factory in London, but when civilian sales failed to take off he closed it again.

Back in Hartford, Colt's business was booming. In 1855 he opened a new and much larger factory that he named The Colt Armory. As several Southern states began to consider leaving the Union, they wanted to build up their militias in case the federal government used force to stop them seceding. Colt sold vast numbers of guns to the Southern states, though that trade was banned once the Civil War actually began. Instead Colt sold guns to the Union army.

By the end of the Civil War, Samuel Colt himself had died, and his patents on revolvers were running out. The company faced a serious crisis in the later 1860s and nearly went under. The company regained prosperity by adapting its designs to take metallic cartridges that were loaded from the rear of the cylinder. By employing a series of talented designers and manufacturers, the Colt Company has never looked back.

1892 NEW NAVY REVOLVER

The 1892 New Navy revolver had a barrel length of 6 inches and was 11 inches overall. It was bought in large numbers by the U.S. Navy, becoming the standard sidearm for officers, and was also available to the public. The blued finish to the steel parts show that this is a military version, as does the .41 caliber. The ring on the end of the handle is for a lanyard that attached the pistol to a belt so that it would not be lost if dropped.

Lanyard ring

Recessed hammer spur

Trigger guard

BILLY THE KID

When the famous outlaw of the Wild West Billy the Kid (1859–81) was finally gunned down, he was carrying a Colt "Thunderer." He first came to the notice of the law in 1877 in Silver City, New Mexico, when he got into an argument with a blacksmith named Cahill and shot him dead. The killer abandoned his real name of William McCarty, adopted that of William Bonney and went on the run. Over the next few years Billy rustled cattle, robbed travelers, moved to Mexico, returned to the United States and became a gunman of deadly accuracy. Exactly how many men Billy the Kid killed is uncertain, though the number is usually put at 21. He was ambushed by Sheriff Pat Garret, who had earlier been a friend, and killed in 1881.

NEW DOUBLE-ACTION REVOLVER

In 1877 Colt produced their first double-action weapon, meaning that pulling the trigger both fired the gun and rotated the cylinder. Officially the weapon was the M1877, but for marketing purposes it was given more exciting names. The .38 version shown above was dubbed the "Lightning," while the .41 variant was named the "Thunderer." Unfortunately the hammer spring had a tendency to break and this affected sales even after the problem had been solved.

"Colt DA 41" etched on barrel

The famous rampant colt logo of the company

COLT .41 DOUBLE-ACTION REVOLVER

The Colt .41 Double-Action revolver, usually shortened to the DA 41, was developed in 1877 to use the new .41-long cartridge. That cartridge had been developed in response to a demand for a bullet with greater stopping power that could still be fired from a conventional revolver. The bullet had a wider caliber than the conventional .38 and a longer case to allow for a greater charge of powder.

COLT OFFICIAL POLICE REVOLVER

At the end of the 19th century, police departments all over America were phasing out the .32 caliber revolvers that had long been standard-issue, replacing them with .38 calibers. To fill this new demand, Colt introduced the Army Special, a modernized revolver that soon became the service revolver for many police departments.

In 1927, Colt made a few superficial changes to the Army Special and redubbed it the "Official Police" model. The marketing ploy was a brilliant success: by the 1930s, big-city departments like New York, Kansas City and Los Angeles equipped their personnel with Colt's revolvers, as did the Treasury Department, Coast Guard, Postal Inspection Service and FBI. Ironically, the Official Police (shown above) was a favored weapon of notorious gangster Al Capone.

The American Civil War

The American Civil War broke out in 1861, a time when pistol design and development was undergoing rapid change. The percussion cap was by now well established, but was in the process of being replaced by cartridges that contained powder, ball and detonator in one package. Similarly the older single-shot or turnover models were being replaced by revolvers that could fire multiple times without reloading, although at this time, they were not always very reliable.

Given the rapid changes taking place, it was hardly surprising that a wide range of different pistol types saw action in the war. This variety was made all the greater by the fact that many officers chose to bring their own pistols to the war rather than to rely on models issued by their state or national governments.

As the war broke out the Confederacy had a clear advantage in terms of numbers and quality of troops. There were large numbers of volunteers—more than the various states could train and equip—while many of these volunteers came carrying their own weapons. The Confederate advantage was especially marked in terms of cavalry, and it was the cavalry that used the pistol far more than the infantry.

Among the weapons brought to war by their owners was the Volcanic repeating pistol, produced by Smith & Wesson. This high-quality .44 caliber rimfire revolver was highly sought after, but only available in small numbers. The Kerr revolver, made in London, was imported to the Confederacy in large numbers. This robust single-action gun held five .44 cartridges and was as reliable as it was simple.

Even the official weapons could include some odd examples. The U.S. Navy, for instance, armed some of its officers with the Elgin pistol. This was a .54 caliber single-shot percussion-cap pistol to which a Bowie knife blade was firmly attached. As time passed the greater wealth of the Northern states began to tell. By 1864 Northern arms factories were producing a range of reliable, heavy-duty pistols that, if not better than their Southern counterparts, were available in much larger numbers.

JEFFERSON DAVIS

President of the Confederate States of America throughout the American Civil War, Jefferson Davis was an able soldier and politician, but a poor diplomat and statesman whose talents and failings became more obvious as the war progressed. Davis was born in Kentucky and grew up in Mississippi. In 1824 he went to West Point, after which he joined the U.S. Army. He fought with distinction in the Black Hawk War of 1832. He then left the army after his prospective father-in-law, future U.S. president Zachary Taylor, made this a condition of his permission to marry.

When the Mexican–American War broke out in 1846, Davis raised a regiment of volunteer infantry and went to war as its colonel (his wife having died). Davis was an acknowledged expert of small arms and insisted his regiment be armed with the M1841 rifle, then a new and relatively untried gun, though as an officer he himself carried a pistol.

After the war, Davis left the army again and started the political career that would see him raised to president of the Confederacy. Unlike his rival president, Abraham Lincoln, Davis had had a distinguished career as soldier when the war broke out.

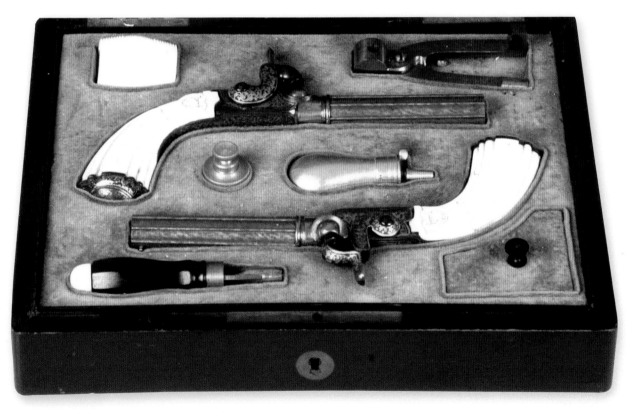

JEFFERSON DAVIS'S PISTOLS

Like most Southern gentlemen of his generation, Jefferson Davis owned a cased pair of pistols. This set, however, was never used by Davis—it was captured by the U.S. Navy as it made its way to him from Belgium.

The magnificent pair of weapons with ivory handles and gold inlay had been intended as a presentation set by European gunsmiths eager to sell their more modern weapons to the Confederacy.

American Civil War Pistols

During the 1860s pistols were comparatively inaccurate weapons, of real use only at short range, which dictated where they were used and by whom. The rank and file of infantry carried muskets or rifles that could be fired over a longer range. Most infantry officers, however, carried pistols. This was partly because their duties meant that they had to spend most of their time watching events around their unit, consulting maps, carrying messages and performing other duties where a long rifle would get in the way. While they were expected to use a pistol or sword for personal protection against the enemy, they were also expected to keep their men in their ranks, and this might include shooting men who ran or panicked in the heat of battle. Cavalry rank and file were more likely to be armed with pistols. These were sometimes of the heavier style that were powerful enough to bring down the horse of an enemy rider with a single shot.

Octagonal barrel

SAVAGE–NORTH REVOLVER

This percussion–cap revolver is unusual in having the caps mounted on the outside of the cylinder, not on its rear, and the hammer striking vertically down. It features two triggers. The lower ring trigger cocks the gun, while the upper trigger fires it. About 11,000 of these pistols were made for the U.S. Army by the Savage Revolving Arms company of Connecticut.

Double trigger in guard

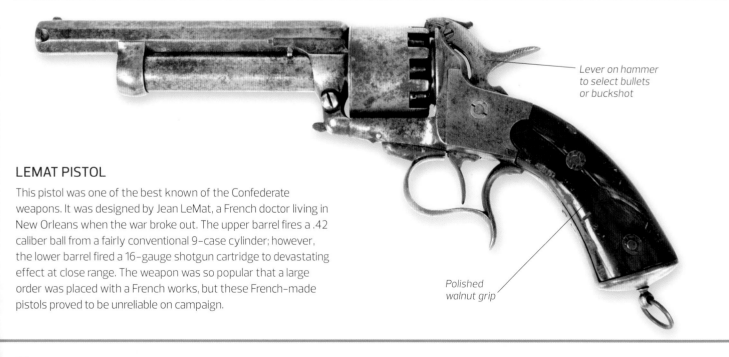

Lever on hammer to select bullets or buckshot

LEMAT PISTOL

This pistol was one of the best known of the Confederate weapons. It was designed by Jean LeMat, a French doctor living in New Orleans when the war broke out. The upper barrel fires a .42 caliber ball from a fairly conventional 9-case cylinder; however, the lower barrel fired a 16-gauge shotgun cartridge to devastating effect at close range. The weapon was so popular that a large order was placed with a French works, but these French-made pistols proved to be unreliable on campaign.

Polished walnut grip

LEFAUCHEUX M1858

French gunsmith Casimir Lefaucheux died in 1852, but his company was still in business when the American Civil War broke out. The M1858, shown here, was chambered for the 12mm pinfire cartridge. It became one the company's leading products and was adopted by the French navy and some cavalry regiments as a standard sidearm. Agents from the federal government bought 12,000 of these for the U.S. Cavalry, which were delivered to New York in 1862. The U.S. government was subsequently unimpressed to find that Lefaucheux was also selling the pistol to the Confederacy, though the French pointed out that they had not signed an exclusive contract.

The hinged gate opened to show a pinfire cartridge partially ejected

STARR REVOLVER

When this model of revolver was first produced by Ebenezer Starr of New York it had a double action. The U.S. Army wanted a single action revolver, however, so Starr quickly altered the mechanism and promptly sold 25,000 to the government. More were sold to various Northern states for use by the militia regiments, and by the end of the war nearly 50,000 Starr Revolvers had been produced.

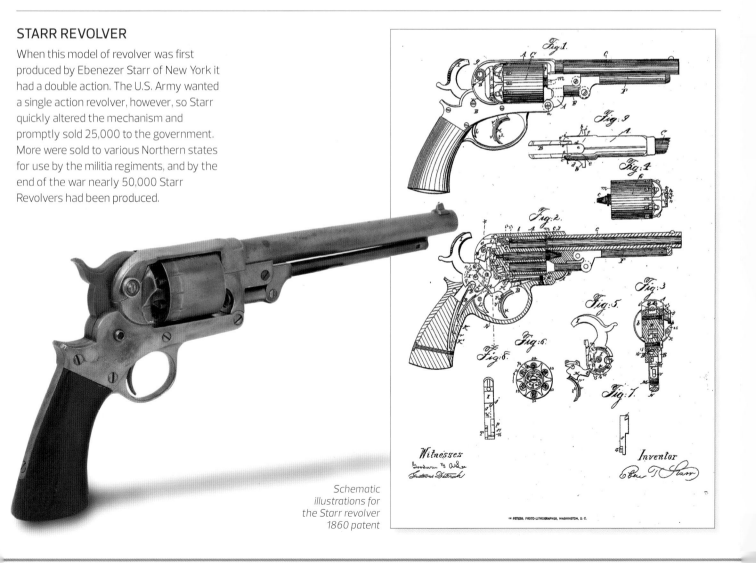

Schematic illustrations for the Starr revolver 1860 patent

Colt's Competitors

Until Colt went into mass production in the 1850s, craftsmen made pistols by hand, each individually made from raw materials. The resulting weapons varied greatly in quality, depending on the skills of the maker.

Colt's system of bulk manufacturing ensured consistency of quality for all its guns. Every gun was made to the same standard with parts from one gun interchangeable with those from another. A customer picking up a Colt knew exactly what he was getting.

Standardization gave Colt a huge commercial advantage, but it was not long before competitors began to copy Colt's methods. The Massachusetts Arms Company was among the first, getting into full production by the 1860s. Smith & Wesson were not far behind, though other companies such as Remington took longer to adopt the new techniques. By the late 19th century, Colt had scores of competitors in America, as well as many In Great Britain and Europe.

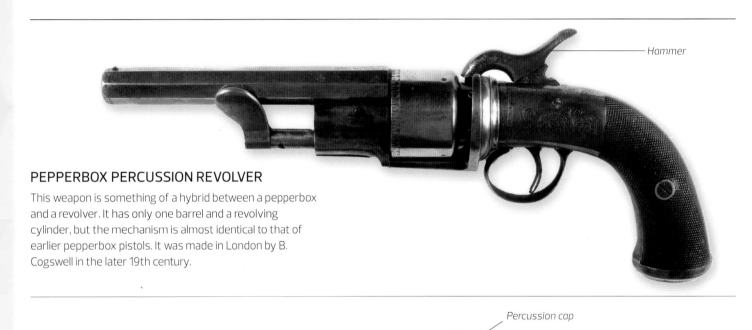

Hammer

PEPPERBOX PERCUSSION REVOLVER

This weapon is something of a hybrid between a pepperbox and a revolver. It has only one barrel and a revolving cylinder, but the mechanism is almost identical to that of earlier pepperbox pistols. It was made in London by B. Cogswell in the later 19th century.

Octagonal barrel

Percussion cap

Bronze grip

Etched floral scrollwork

COGSWELL TRANSITION GUN

This gun by London gunsmith B. Cogswell has a six-shot cylinder firing .44 caliber balls and was made in about 1850. The individual chambers are loaded with powder and ball by hand, then fired by a percussion cap. The fact that there is only one hammer and nipple makes this a slower gun to repeat fire than a true revolver with a nipple and cap on each chamber.

MASSACHUSETTS ARMS COMPANY .28

The Massachusetts Arms Company was founded in 1850 by Arthur Savage, Horace Smith and Daniel Wesson. At first it produced revolvers, until it lost a court case with Colt, after which it concentrated on rifles and carbines. The company did, however, produce a number of pistols, such as this .28 six-shot example designed by Edward Maynard. Maynard had developed a system by which a roll of paper impregnated with fulminate took the place of the percussion cap. The action of turning the cylinder advanced the paper roll so that a new patch of fulminate covered the nipple. This gave a higher rate of fire, but was prone to malfunction.

MASSACHUSETTS ARMS CASED SET

Higher-quality pistols were sold as cased sets together with matching accessories. This Wesson and Leavitt pistol was made by the Massachusetts Arms Company in about 1850. As well as the revolver, the box contains a bullet mold, rammer, powder flask (embellished with an eagle design), percussion caps and cleaning cloth.

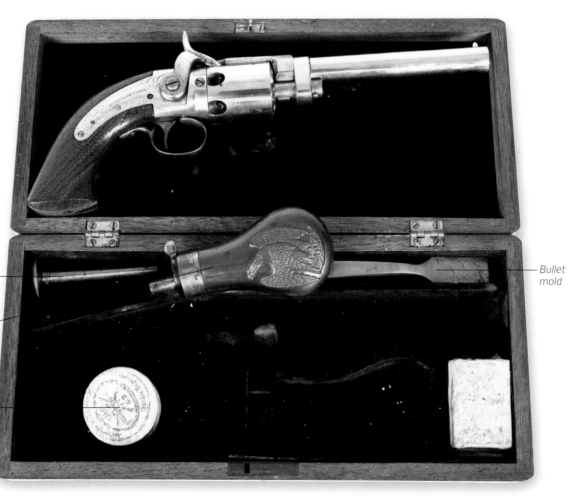

Brass rammer

Powder flask

Caps

Bullet mold

Gemstones of various colors embedded in handle

IMITATION COLT REVOLVER

The commercial success of the Colt Company's guns encouraged many others to mimic them. Colt fought numerous lawsuits to enforce its patents, but those patents were not recognized in all countries. This copy of a .38 Colt double–action revolver, which Colt had introduced in 1892, was made in Spain during the 1920s. The wooden handle has been embellished with some small gemstones.

FROM PERCUSSION CAP TO METALLIC CARTRIDGE

Although the percussion-cap system had many advantages over the old flintlock system, it was still a fairly slow way of loading a gun. The barrel, or chamber of a revolver cylinder, had to be loaded by hand with gunpowder, ball and finally a wad to keep everything in place. This then had to be rammed down hard to get the best explosive power from the loose powder. The percussion cap had replaced the flint and loose powder of the flintlock, but that was all.

For centuries ammunition had been supplied in the form of a paper cartridge, which contained a measured amount of gunpowder and the ball. To load a gun, the user first bit the end off the cartridge and poured the gunpowder down the barrel. The ball was dropped in next, followed by the screwed–up paper to act as a wad. The first successful attempt to use the cartridge without tearing it open came with the needle gun developed by German gunsmith Johann Dreyse in 1836. The Dreyse cartridge was a paper packet containing not only powder and ball, but also a percussion explosive located between the powder and ball. When the gun was fired, a needle penetrated the cartridge from behind, lancing through the powder to hit and detonate the explosive. This set off the gunpowder and so fired the gun.

To work effectively, the needle gun had to be loaded from the breech end so that the paper cartridge remained intact until fired. The method chosen by Dreyse to open the breech of his barrel was a bolt action. The cartridge was placed into the rear of the barrel, after which a bolt was pushed forward to close the breech, and twisted half a turn to lock an interrupted screw thread that held it securely in place while the gun was fired. The bolt was then twisted the other way and drawn back to repeat the process.

The main weakness of the system was that the paper cartridge would often leave fragments in the breech that were difficult to clean out in combat. In 1846 French gunsmith Benjamin Houllier produced a cartridge that replaced paper with copper. The copper jacket was left behind when the bullet was fired, but was much easier to remove than burnt paper scraps. The copper jacket was also more robust when being handled prior to firing.

THE CARTRIDGE PISTOL

Another potential challenge to Colt came from the introduction of fully enclosed metallic cartridges. In the mid-1850s, Americans Horace Smith and Daniel Wesson, who had pioneered both the metallic cartridge and the repeating rifle, developed a revolver firing rimfire cartridges that was based on a cylinder design purchased from a former Colt employee, Rollin White. (According to some sources, White first offered his innovative design to Samuel Colt, but with an uncharacteristic failure of foresight, Colt didn't think metallic cartridges had any potential.) Smith & Wesson put its pistol, in a .22 model, on the market in 1857, after Colt's patents had expired.

The combat advantages of a revolver that could load cartridges quickly—as opposed to the slow-loading cap-and-ball system used by Colt and others—were obvious, and a .32 version proved popular with Union forces during the Civil War. But again, Colt's dominance was not seriously challenged, because S&W's production was not fast enough to keep up with demand, both in pistols and in ammunition. In the last years of the conflict, Colt revolvers did face a serious competitor in the form of the Remington Model 1863 Army revolver. While still a cap-and-ball weapon, many soldiers found it to be easier to load and fire than its Colt counterparts. When S&W's patent expired in 1872, Colt and a host of other gunmakers rushed to get their own cartridge revolvers on the market

Sliding sleeve moves forward

SLOCUM REVOLVER

General Henry Slocum was born in Brooklyn, New York, and successfully led troops from that state in the American Civil War. When the Brooklyn Arms Company introduced this revolver in 1863, it named the weapon The Slocum after the general. The gun had an ingenious sliding tube mechanism that allowed each cartridge to be ejected after firing.

Varnished rosewood grips

REMINGTON NEW MODEL ARMY

In 1858 the Remington Company introduced the New Model Army, frequently referred to as the Model 1858, as that date is stamped on the barrel. It is a single-action revolver, meaning that the trigger performs only the single action of firing the gun. The cylinder is advanced between shots by manually pulling back the hammer. More than 150,000 examples were made of this percussion-cap gun, many of them later converted to cartridge action.

Engraved lock plate

Stud trigger

ALLEN & WHEELOCK PISTOL

Produced in 1858 by celebrated gunsmith Ethan Allen in partnership with Thomas Wheelock, this pistol was an effort to get around the patents held by Sam Colt. The ammunition was of the Allen-developed lipfire configuration, and the cylinder moved on a rack-and-pinion device. Neither innovation proved to be successful.

SMITH AND WESSON

In 1855 gunsmiths Horace Smith and Daniel Wesson left the company they had been working for to set up on their own. The two men purchased from inventor Rollin White the patent for a revolving cylinder that contained chambers to take metallic cartridges, loaded from behind—a patent previously spurned by Samuel Colt—and began production in Springfield, Massachusetts.

At the same time, the new company produced the Smith & Wesson Cartridge No. 1, a metal cartridge using the rimfire system that was cheap to make and reliable in use.

Thereafter the Smith & Wesson company has concentrated on reliable firearms of modest cost, together with the development of a range of ammunition types to be used in its own and other firearms.

Horace Smith   *Daniel B. Wesson*

Smith & Wesson factory, Springfield, Massachusetts (c. 1908)

Among the cartridges developed have been the .38 S&W, first made in 1877 and which remains in production in small numbers. The .38 S&W was for over 30 years the main revolver ammunition used by the British army. More recent has been the S&W .500 Magnum, which entered production in 2003. This cartridge is the most powerful handgun cartridge in the world and, at the time of its introduction, was so powerful that no existing pistol could use it. The .500 Magnum is used by hunters as an ammunition to use in pistols in case of a large-animal attack.

In 1964 the Wesson family sold the company to an industrial conglomerate, and it has gone through other changes of ownership since. It remains based in Springfield, where it began its life.

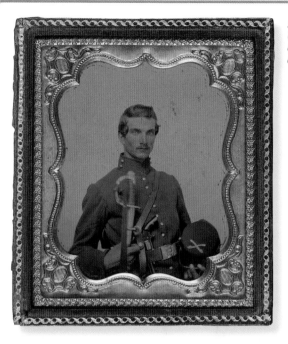

American Civil War soldier in Union uniform holding kepi with cavalry insignia, cavalry saber, and Smith & Wesson revolver

SMITH & WESSON NO. 2

The fortunes of the Smith & Wesson company was founded on its No. 2 Revolver, which was first produced in 1861. The timing proved to be fortuitous because the American Civil War broke out that same year, leading to a huge demand for firearms. The No. 2 proved to be especially popular with Union cavalry officers, and for a while the company had trouble producing enough weapons to keep up with demand. The cylinder was removed for reloading by unclipping the barrel so that it would swivel upwards. It was available with a 4-, 5- or 6-inch barrel and with a blued or nickel finish. Both finishes were designed to inhibit rust, a prime consideration for a soldier on campaign.

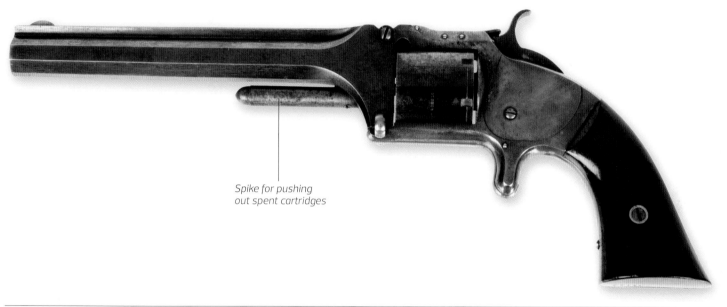

Spike for pushing out spent cartridges

Stud trigger

MOORE POCKET REVOLVER

A pocket revolver produced by Daniel Moore in the 1860s. In an effort to get around the patents held by Smith & Wesson, Moore developed the teat-fire cartridge. Instead of having a flat base, the teat-fire had a rounded base with a protruding teat. The cartridges were loaded into the cylinder from the front, with the teat protruding from the back to be hit by the hammer. Around 30,000 of these small guns were produced before the patent was bought by the Colt Company in 1870.

BELGIAN REVOLVER

This revolver was made in Belgium in the middle of the 19th century. It was designed to operate on the pinfire system. This cartridge had a pin projecting from the side of the base. When the pin was hit by the hammer it crushed the primer against the opposite side of the cartridge, which was backed by the side of the barrel, thus firing the gun. The system went out of production when reliable rimfire and centerfire cartridges were developed.

Six-shot cylinder

Pinfire mechanism

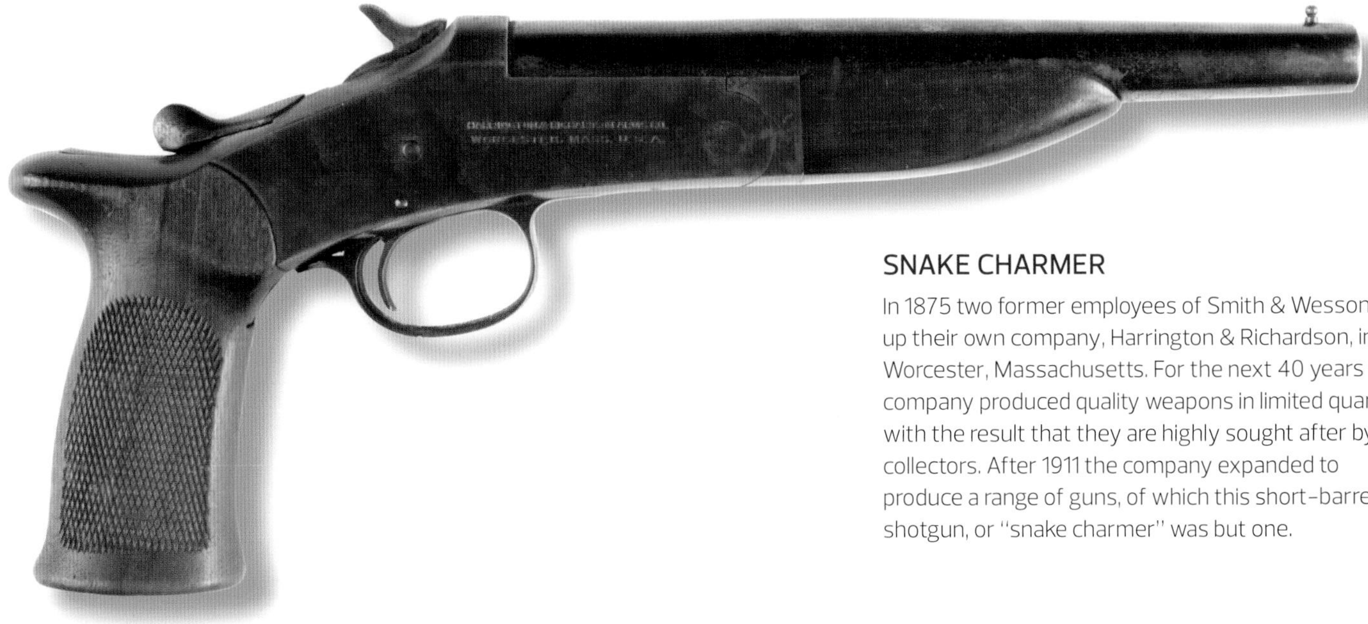

SNAKE CHARMER

In 1875 two former employees of Smith & Wesson set up their own company, Harrington & Richardson, in Worcester, Massachusetts. For the next 40 years the company produced quality weapons in limited quantity, with the result that they are highly sought after by collectors. After 1911 the company expanded to produce a range of guns, of which this short-barreled shotgun, or "snake charmer" was but one.

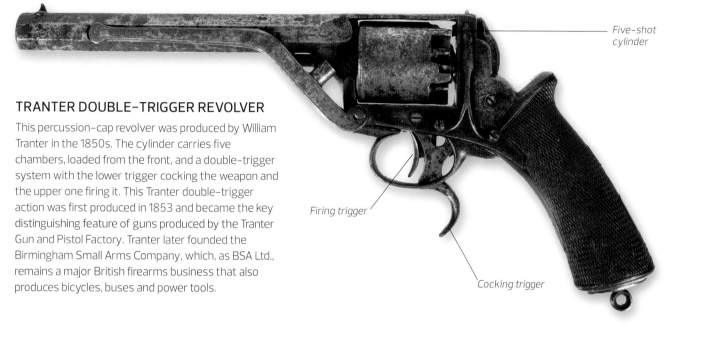

Five-shot cylinder

TRANTER DOUBLE-TRIGGER REVOLVER

This percussion-cap revolver was produced by William Tranter in the 1850s. The cylinder carries five chambers, loaded from the front, and a double-trigger system with the lower trigger cocking the weapon and the upper one firing it. This Tranter double-trigger action was first produced in 1853 and became the key distinguishing feature of guns produced by the Tranter Gun and Pistol Factory. Tranter later founded the Birmingham Small Arms Company, which, as BSA Ltd., remains a major British firearms business that also produces bicycles, buses and power tools.

Firing trigger

Cocking trigger

Ejector mechanism

WILLIAMS AND POWELL REVOLVER

Williams and Powell was a firearms company in Liverpool, England, during the mid-19th century. The company produced guns designed by the renowned Robert Adams and his brother, John. For many years in the later 19th century, the British army adopted the Adams Patent Revolver, putting out manufacturing to a number of different companies. This example, however, seems to have been made for the civilian market, as it carries no government marks.

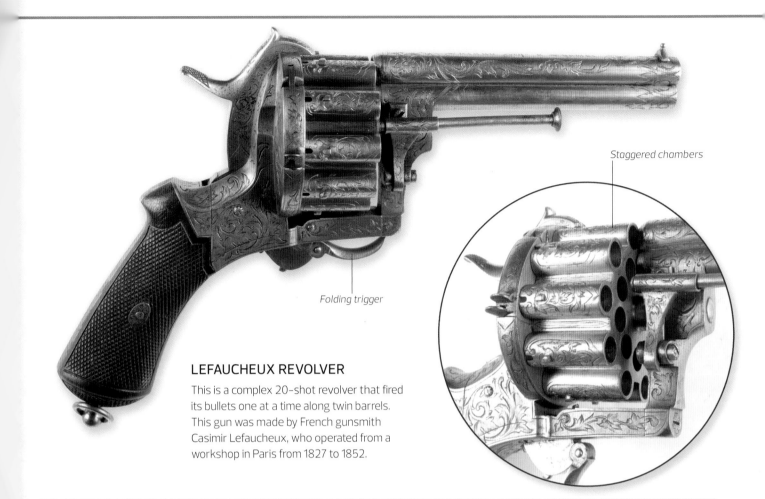

Staggered chambers

Folding trigger

LEFAUCHEUX REVOLVER

This is a complex 20-shot revolver that fired its bullets one at a time along twin barrels. This gun was made by French gunsmith Casimir Lefaucheux, who operated from a workshop in Paris from 1827 to 1852.

GENERAL GEORGE ARMSTRONG CUSTER

One of the most controversial commanders in American military history, Custer achieved remarkable feats, but his entire career was overshadowed by his death in battle against Native Americans. Custer graduated last of his class from West Point in 1861, but his dashing and successful actions as a U.S. Army cavalry commander during the American Civil War brought him to the rank of major general by 1865. Custer's success was based on careful scouting of the enemy position and strength combined with his own sound tactical sense of where to launch a charge.

When the war ended Custer reverted to his permanent rank of captain and spent several years on mundane duties before being given command of the 7th Cavalry and being sent west to campaign in the Indian Wars. In 1876 Custer and the 7th Cavalry were sent as part of a larger campaign to defeat the combined forces of the Lakota, Cheyenne and Arapaho. Custer found the main tribal camp on the Little Big Horn River and attacked. Custer divided his force to attack the camp from two directions. The southern attack, under Major Reno, was halted and took heavy casualties. Custer led the northern assault, but he and all his 208 men were killed.

Custer holding a revolver as a West Point cadet, c. 1860

Whenever he rode to battle, Custer took pistols. A witness who saw him ride to the Little Big Horn said he wore "two self-cocking, white-handled British pistols." Yet, Custer did not own any such weapons. He did, however, own a pair of pearl-handled Smith & Wesson No. 2 pistols, so he may have taken those into his last battle.

MANUAL REVOLVER

This fine percussion-cap weapon from the 1850s has some advanced features. The rod under the barrel swings down to operate a ram that compresses the ball and powder in the cylinder. The spur under the trigger guard allows a finger to steady the gun while firing.

Trigger sits behind hammer

Scrollwork of spiraling leaves embellish the frame

Ejector rod

BELGIAN REVOLVER

A simple, small percussion-cap revolver made in Belgium in the middle of the 19th century. It is unadorned and in places is crudely finished, indicating that it is a cheaply produced piece.

BELGIAN REVOLVER

Over 300,000 official versions of the extremely popular French Model 1873 Army revolver were manufactured, plus an unknown number of unofficial copies. The pistol was officially replaced by the Model 1892, but it was so rugged that it was brought back into service in the trenches of World War I and was given to reservists in 1939. This example is a copy made in Belgium in about 1890.

Octagonal barrel

The carved leaves that decorate the handle are a nonstandard embellishment.

FRANCO-PRUSSIAN WAR

When the Franco-Prussian War broke out in July 1870 both France and Prussia were supremely confident of achieving a swift victory. The French believed in offensive spirit, initiative and morale. The Prussians put their faith in discipline, training and massed numbers. The Prussians won a stunning victory, and armies around the world settled down to learn the lessons. Clear lines of command, conscription and good supply systems had played a large part in Prussian victory, but so too had weaponry. Most armies realized that a sword was useless to an infantry officer—though they were retained for ceremonial use—so pistols began to be widely issued in their place. Thus it was that the years 1875 to 1895 saw a rapid development in robust military pistols designed to function in muddy, wet, dry, cold and hot conditions.

Les dernières cartouches (*The last cartridges*) by Alphonse de Neuville, known for intensely patriotic paintings of the Franco-Prussian and other wars. Here he depicts French snipers ambushing Bavarian troops, hiding in the l'Auberge Bourgerie in Bazeilles, prior to the Battle of Sedan in 1870.

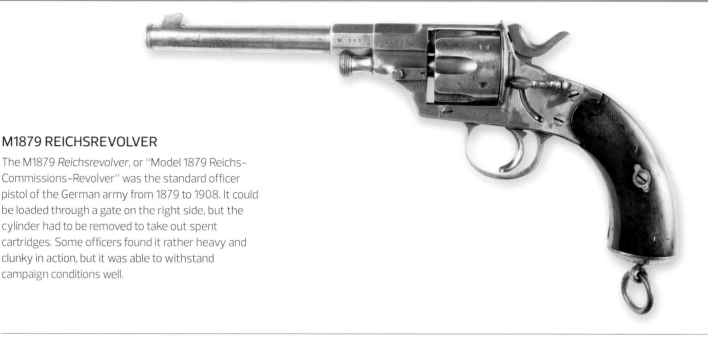

M1879 REICHSREVOLVER

The M1879 *Reichsrevolver*, or "Model 1879 Reichs-Commissions-Revolver" was the standard officer pistol of the German army from 1879 to 1908. It could be loaded through a gate on the right side, but the cylinder had to be removed to take out spent cartridges. Some officers found it rather heavy and clunky in action, but it was able to withstand campaign conditions well.

Latch for hinged frame

DANISH DOUBLE-ACTION PISTOL

In 1876 Belgian gunsmith Jean-Baptiste Ronge filed a patent for this revolver, which has a hinged frame that breaks forward for loading and unloading the cylinder. The Danish armed forces were looking for a new officer pistol and ordered large numbers from Ronge. Those destined for the Danish military had a lanyard ring added to the handle and were stamped DENMARK on top of the frame. Those sold to civilian users lacked both features but were otherwise identical.

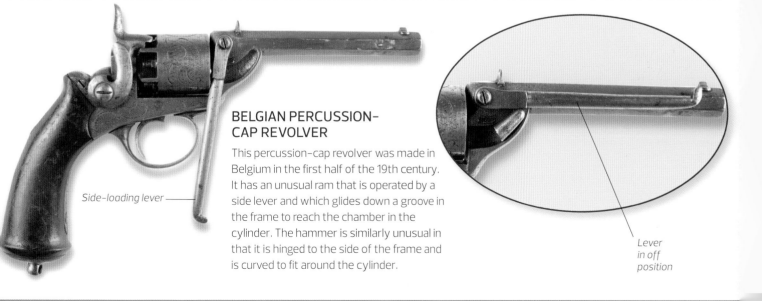

BELGIAN PERCUSSION-CAP REVOLVER

This percussion-cap revolver was made in Belgium in the first half of the 19th century. It has an unusual ram that is operated by a side lever and which glides down a groove in the frame to reach the chamber in the cylinder. The hammer is similarly unusual in that it is hinged to the side of the frame and is curved to fit around the cylinder.

Side-loading lever

Lever in off position

Cylinder

Subtle floral etching
adds interest to frame

TIPPING AND LAWDEN BLACK METAL REVOLVER

This unusual cast-steel revolver was made by Birmingham-based Tipping and Lawden, which had a factory on Constitution Hill. They made a variety of revolvers, this being the "Thomas Patent 158" model. The company later joined with others in the city to form Birmingham Small Arms Company, which is still trading. The pistol is stamped "John Clarke, Newton Abbot," this presumably being the name and hometown of the owner.

Hammer spur

Model number
engraved into
the other side.

HUSQVARNA 1433 REVOLVER

The Swedish company Husqvarna is today better known for its power tools, but it began life in the 18th century manufacturing small arms, such as this Model 1433 revolver from the late 19th century. Husqvarna was originally an arsenal, making weapons for the military. After the Franco-Prussian War, though, its style of precision, lightweight weapons was no longer wanted by the military. Husqvarna then moved into the civilian market. The company ceased production of firearms in 1968.

Eight-shot cylinder

Ejector rod

RAST & GASSER M1898 REVOLVER

The Rast & Gasser M1898 was a solid-frame, double-action revolver that was the standard officer's pistol of the Austro-Hungarian army from its introduction in 1898 to the collapse of the empire in 1918. Well over 200,000 were made by the time production ceased. This, together with its robust and reliable form, meant that it was still in use with various Balkan armies during World War II, and a few are still used today.

L-shaped grip

Trigger guard

Front of
trigger guard

Center pin

Original
position
of barrel

Hinge

Release button

Release button

CAST-STEEL REVOLVER

This .44 revolver made in Belgium has a rather unusual break mechanism to allow loading and unloading. A clip on the trigger guard is moved to the right, allowing the barrel and cylinder to swing upward around a hinge above the firing hammer. The pistol, marked "9990" on the barrel, was made in the 1870s, with this example being exported to Britain.

Pistols of the American West

Few eras of history have been so often represented, and misrepresented, in fictional novels and movies as the American West in the years 1865 to 1900. In popular imagination, all men in the West were cowboys, wore big hats and carried six-shooter revolvers. Beguiling as the image may be, the truth was rather more complicated. There were cowboys in plenty, but there were also miners, farmers, soldiers and storekeepers. Only a minority of men habitually carried a gun, as most simply did not need one for their everyday existence. That said, guns were carried more frequently and more openly in the 19th-century West than today, and some of those weapons have rightly entered both history and legend.

Ejector rod

Double barrel

Cylinder stores twenty bullets

"WILD WEST" REVOLVER

Manufactured by Henrion, Dassy and Heuschen in Belgium, this revolver was marketed under the name of "Wild West," although it did not enter production until 1910. It has two barrels, one above the other, while the cylinder holds 20 6.5mm cartridges arranged in two circles. It therefore had nothing to do with the real American West, but is a tribute to how that era had taken a hold on the public imagination in a foreign country so quickly.

BELLE STAR REVOLVER

Very much a real weapon of the Wild West is this Navy Model pistol from the Manhattan Firearms Company. The gun is a near copy of the Colt Navy revolver, produced after Colt's patents ran out.

Notorious outlaw Belle Starr owned this particular example. Born in Missouri, after the Civil War, Starr moved to Texas, where her husband was a known rustler. After his death she married Cherokee Bill Starr and set up as a handler of stolen goods and livestock. Despite a short spell in prison, Starr and her husband ran a highly successful outlaw gang until February 1889, when she was shot dead. The killer was never caught, but was believed to be her son, Eddie, whom she had beaten mercilessly when he was a child.

Rammer lever

Rammer pivot pin

Brass

ADAMS REVOLVER

This percussion-cap revolver was manufactured by British gunsmith Robert Adams in the 1860s. Adams was born in 1809 and for most of his career worked for the George & John Deane company in London. By 1851 the company had become Deane and Adams to reflect the importance of Adams's design work, becoming Deane, Adams and Deane when another generation of the Deane family joined. It was Adams who invented the first double-action revolver, later selling large numbers to the British army and in America. Compared to its main rival in the West, the Adams gun was more accurate and lighter, but more expensive and less powerful. Adams continued to improve and refine his revolver designs until his death in 1880.

The Automatic Pistol

Many gunsmiths relied upon the revolver mechanism to produce a pistol that could be fired several times without stopping to reload, while others turned to what became known as the semiautomatic action.

A semiautomatic pistol uses the recoil of the fired gun to power a mechanism that ejects the spent cartridge and moves a new cartridge into the firing chamber ready to be fired. Gunmakers began working in earnest on this system in the 1890s, by which time reliable metal cartridges were being produced in large numbers.

The majority of semiautomatic pistols are double action, meaning that as the trigger is pulled it first cocks the hammer and then releases it to fire the gun. A smaller number of models are single action, requiring the hammer to be cocked independently before the trigger is pulled to fire the weapon.

BORCHARDT PISTOL

The first gunsmith to produce a commercially successful semiautomatic pistol was the German Hugo Borchardt with his C-93. The weapon was immediately successful, with more than 3,000 being produced. To make the weapon work properly, Borchardt developed his own cartridge, the 7.65 x 25mm, which gave enough power to work the reloading mechanism. The gun featured several innovations, of which perhaps the longest lasting was the fact that the eight-round magazine was loaded into the handle. The pistol used a toggle-lock, meaning that as it was fired a two-piece arm rose and flexed to open the breech and allow the used cartridge to leave. The weapon failed to capture the military market, although it was tested in both the United States and Switzerland, due to its powerful recoil and awkward weight distribution.

Recoil-spring housing with rear sight on top

Butt holds moveable eight-round magazine

BERGMANN SEMIAUTOMATIC

German gunsmith Theodor Bergmann produced a number of semiautomatic pistols in the 1890s, this being the 1893 model. Although they differed in detail, all models shared some characteristics. The guns had an internal box magazine in front of the trigger that held five cartridges and a barrel 4 inches long. The guns were comparatively light and handy, weighing only just over 2 pounds. The spent cartridges were ejected by the pressure of the gas they themselves created when fired. The pistol did not achieve high sales, so Bergmann turned to fully automatic weapons and found great success with the MP18.

Rounds fed from magazine forward of trigger guard

Revolver-style grip

8-inch barrel

ARTILLERY LUGER

In 1908 Georg Luger designed what was first called the Long Pistol Model 1908, but later became known as the Artillery Luger after it was adopted by the German army as a sidearm for artillery men. This version of the basic Luger had an 8-inch barrel and came with a detachable 32-round magazine that fitted on to the base of the grip. The sights were calibrated up to 800 yards, indicating the much greater accuracy of the longer barrel. For added range, the pistol came with a wooden shoulder stock that clipped onto the grip and allowed it to be used as a carbine.

Bottom of grip accepts a shoulder stock

Toggle doubles as cocking grip

Safety catch

4-inch barrel

LUGER P08

When the Deutsche Waffen und Munitionsfabriken (DWM) company became dissatisfied with the Borchardt C-93, they asked Borchardt to make modifications. Borchardt refused, so the company called in designer Georg Luger to do the work instead. The family of weapons that resulted quickly became known as "Lugers," though the design owed as much to Borchardt as to Luger. This is P08 model, which was adopted as the standard sidearm for officers in the German army in 1908 and retained that role through to 1945.

10-round removable magazine

Magazine catch

GEORG LUGER

Born in 1849, Georg Luger was raised in Steinach am Brenner in Austrian Tyrol, as the son of a provincial doctor and his Italian wife. He showed academic promise at a young age and so was sent to attend secondary school in Padua, Italy, sponsored by his mother's family.

At the age of 18 Luger moved to the Vienna Commercial School, where he learned business management and modern industrial techniques. He passed with distinction, but preferred a military career to an industrial one and so volunteered as an officer cadet in the Austrian 78th Infantry Regiment. He achieved rapid promotion and within just a year was a regular officer with the rank of ensign. It was, however, his superlative marksmanship that got him noticed, and he was then moved to the army's central training school, where he taught shooting and gun maintenance.

After leaving the army, Luger resumed a career in industry working for a variety of engineering companies. Firearms remained a hobby for Luger, but it was not until he joined DWM in 1891 that he began designing them. The famous Luger pistol was his greatest work, appearing in 1904. Luger left DWM in 1918 after a dispute over who owned certain patents, and he died in 1923.

JOHN BROWNING

John Moses Browning was born the son of a gun repair smith in Utah in 1855. He helped in his father's business as a boy, and at the age of 13 he made his first gun, By age 24, he had gained his first patent. He is now recognized as one of the most important gunsmiths of all time, being particularly important to the development of semiautomatic and automatic weapons. In 1885 he began a long collaboration with the Winchester Arms Company, for which he produced a wide range of gun designs utilizing his inventions such as the telescoping bolt and versions of the lever action and pump action. As was usual, Browning sold his designs to Winchester for a cash fee, but in 1898 he asked instead for a royalty payment for each gun sold. Winchester refused and the partnership ended. Browning later led a more nomadic life as he traveled around selling licenses to manufacture his designs. He died in Belgium in 1926.

BROWNING PATENT PISTOL

In 1898 John Browning went on an extended tour of Europe to sell licenses to manufacture his designs. When in Belgium he collaborated with FN Herstal to produce a series of semiautomatic pistols. Although the first of these entered production in 1900, the basic pattern had been designed in about 1896 but had not gone into production in the United States. This example is the FN M1910, one of the last to be produced. It remained in production until 1983.

BROWNING GP HI-POWER

John Browning's collaboration with FN Herstal in Belgium continued for many years. In November 1926 he was at the workbench of his son's design workshop working on a design for a new 9mm semiautomatic pistol for FN Herstal when he suffered a heart attack and fell dead. The design was continued by Dieudonne Saive and eventually entered the market in 1935 as the FN GP35, shown here. The GP element of the name stands for *Grande Puissance*, or "High Power." The model is widely referred to as the Hi-Power in English-speaking countries, though it has always been officially designated the GP.

FN MODÈLE 1906 PISTOL

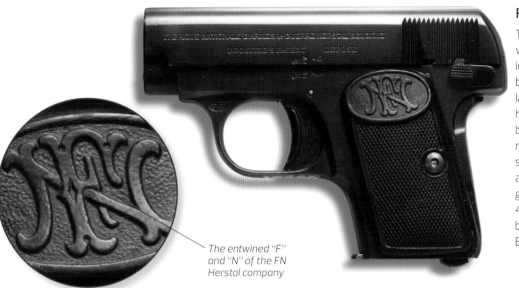

This little pistol is one of several weapons that were made in near-identical versions in the United States by Colt and in Europe by FN Herstal. In later life John Browning refused to sell his designs to arms manufacturers, but instead licensed them in return for royalty payments for each weapon sold. This gun is only 4½ inches long and weighs less than a pound. The gun remained in production for over 40 years, with almost half a million being sold. An improved version, the Baby Browning, remains in production.

The entwined "F" and "N" of the FN Herstal company

FN BDA REVOLVER

The durability of Browning's designs is demonstrated by the FN BDA, shown here. This weapon entered production in 1983 and is used by the Finnish army. From the outside the gun looks modern and has several features to make it better fit the hand and to be easier to place in, and remove from, military-style webbing and holsters. Internally, however, it is virtually indistinguishable from the Browning GP Hi-Power.

Double-action trigger

GENERAL WILLIAM CROZIER

In 1900 the U.S. Army bought a number of German semiautomatic pistols, which were then used in the Moro Rebellion in the Philippines against Islamic rebels. The pistols soon proved to be ineffective against the rebels, who fought guerilla-style, charging out of cover at short range and ignoring wounds that would have stopped less fanatical fighters. The Americans discarded their German pistols in favor of older revolvers that fired a heavier slug and so could stop a Moro tribesman. Chief of Ordnance General William Crozier issued a request for arms companies to submit an automatic firing a cartridge of at least .45 caliber that was capable of sustained firing without malfunction in field trials designed to reproduce campaign conditions. At the special trials held in 1906 every single pistol failed the tests. It was not until 1911 that a weapon was found that matched Crozier's standards. That weapon was the Colt M1911 designed by John Browning.

GAVRIL PRINCIP

Possibly the world's most destructive use of a pistol came on June 28, 1914, when Serb terrorist Gavril Princip shot dead the Austrian Archduke Franz Ferdinand and his wife, Sophia. In 1908 the Austro-Hungarian Empire had annexed Bosnia from the Ottoman Empire. The move disappointed the Serb population of Bosnia, who had hoped that the kingdom of Serbia would seize the province from the ailing Ottoman Empire instead. Serb extremists decided to kill Franz Ferdinand, heir to the Austro-Hungarian throne, on a visit to the Bosnian capital of Sarajevo. Six assassins took up positions along the route to be taken by the Archduke. Five of them bungled their attacks, but Gavril Princip ran forward as the car passed him and fired twice, killing the Archduke and his wife. The pistol he used was an FN M1910. Once Serb involvement became clear, Austria declared war on Serbia and so began World War I, which was to claim over 30 million lives.

Grip safety

Single-action trigger

FN MODÈLE 1910 PISTOL

The pistol used by Gavril Princip was a semiautomatic pistol manufactured in FN Herstal of Belgium to a design by John Browning and supplied to him by the Serb military. The pistol fired .380 ammunition from a six-round magazine in the handle and operated on the blowback mechanism. The design was one of the first to feature a grip safety, meaning that the safety catch is released when the handle is gripped and re-engages as soon as the gun is put down.

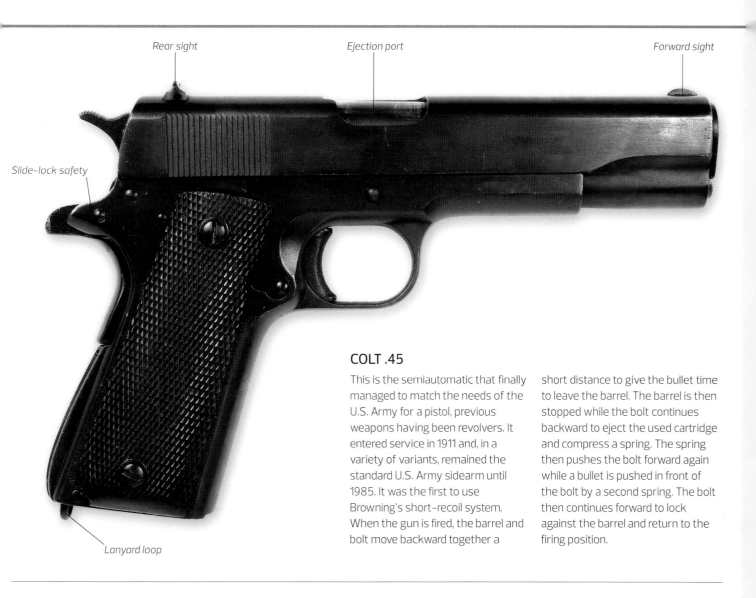

Rear sight

Ejection port

Forward sight

Slide-lock safety

Lanyard loop

COLT .45

This is the semiautomatic that finally managed to match the needs of the U.S. Army for a pistol, previous weapons having been revolvers. It entered service in 1911 and, in a variety of variants, remained the standard U.S. Army sidearm until 1985. It was the first to use Browning's short-recoil system. When the gun is fired, the barrel and bolt move backward together a short distance to give the bullet time to leave the barrel. The barrel is then stopped while the bolt continues backward to eject the used cartridge and compress a spring. The spring then pushes the bolt forward again while a bullet is pushed in front of the bolt by a second spring. The bolt then continues forward to lock against the barrel and return to the firing position.

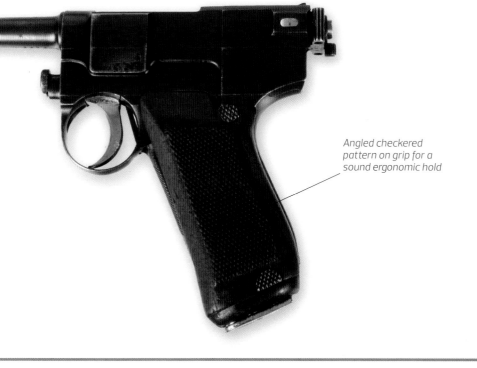

Forward iron sight

Angled checkered pattern on grip for a sound ergonomic hold

GLISENTI M1910

The Glisenti M1910 was the standard sidearm of the Italian army from 1910 to 1945. In 1906 the army decided to replace the aging Bodeo Model 1889 revolver with a new semiautomatic pistol. The design competition was won by Bethel Abiel Revelli, working for the Società Siderurgica Glisenti of Turin. The 1906 model was altered in 1910 to take a 9mm cartridge, and this is the model shown here. The body of the pistol was weaker than comparable designs, however, so it fired only the purpose-made 9 x 19mm Glisenti cartridge that had a smaller charge and therefore less stopping power than others.

BROOMHANDLE MAUSER

Widely known as the "Broomhandle Mauser" because of its shape, this gun is officially named the C96. It was introduced in 1896, in the early days of semiautomatic actions, and continuously refined until it went out of production in 1937. With its relatively long barrel, powerful 7.63 x 25mm cartridge and clip-on shoulder stock, the C96 was accurate to over 200 yards. The box cartridge in front of the barrel could hold 10 cartridges. This combination of features made it a popular choice for army officers, who could afford to equip themselves instead of relying on official firearms.

Tangent (sliding) rear sight

Hammer

Blade forward sight

10 rounds held in box magazine

Distinctive "broomhandle"' design of grip

The Battle of Omdurman

A young Winston Churchill in the uniform of the Fourth Queen's Own Hussars

THE ANGLO–SUDAN WAR'S BATTLE OF OMDURMAN

As the Battle of Omdurman drew to a close on September 2, 1898, British commander Horatio Herbert Kitchener ordered 350 men of the 21st Lancers to ride out in pursuit of the retreating Sudanese army to stop them from occupying the city of Omdurman itself. Seeing 200 Sudanese infantry making for the city, the cavalry charged only to find another 3,000 Sudanese waiting in a gully behind. After a desperate struggle the lancers managed to extricate themselves. In the thick of the action, armed with a Mauser C96, was Lieutenant Winston Churchill, later to be famous as Britain's prime minister in World War II.

SCHWARZLOSE 1908

Designed by Austrian Andreas Schwarzlose, the Schwarzlose 1908 had a highly unusual blow–forward semiautomatic action. As the bullet traveled forward along the barrel, it dragged the barrel forward against a spring. When the spring pushed the barrel back again, it stripped the top cartridge from the magazine in the grip and chambered it ready for firing. Production stopped in 1911, after which the company turned to machine guns.

Frame is marked that it was made in Berlin by A. W. Schwarzlose.

LAHTI L–35

The L–35 was produced in Finland for its army and as a consequence had features that were designed to keep it operating in intensely cold conditions. The most useful of these proved to be the accelerate bolt, which also reduced problems with jammed cartridges. The weapon entered service in 1935 and was used throughout Finland's wars with the Soviet Union in the 1940s. As part of the peace treaty signed by Finland in 1945, the designer, Aimo Lahti, was banned from designing weapons for the rest of his life.

Personal-Defense Weapons

Weapons for personal defense have been carried since the dawn of time. Mostly these have been edged weapons of one kind or another, but as pistols became cheaper in the 19th century, the use of firearms for protection increased. Of particular use are weapons capable of concealed carry, meaning that they are small enough to be carried about the person without being obvious at first glance.

COACHING PISTOL

This twin-barreled percussion-cap pistol has an ingenious firing system. On the end of the hammer is a small rotating disk carrying the striker. Once one barrel has been fired, the disk is rotated to bring the striker into line with the second percussion cap to fire the second barrel. It also has a blade secreted inside the central divide between the barrels that flicks out when a spring release is pressed. Weapons of this sort were carried by men traveling by horse-drawn coach, hence its name.

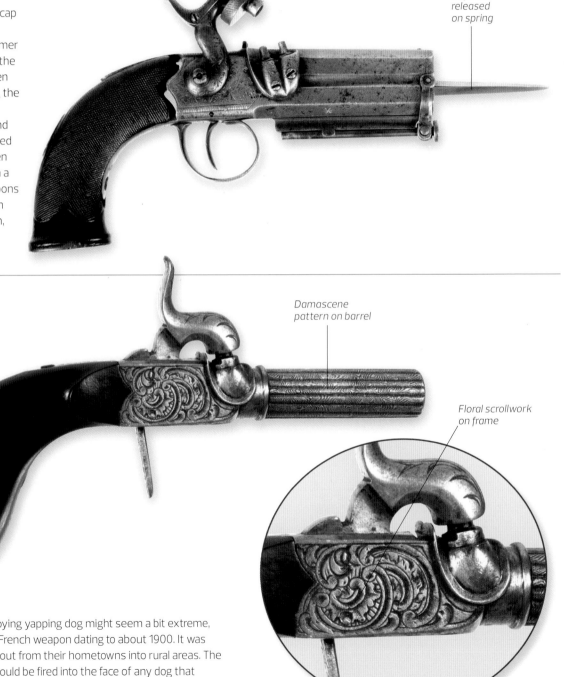

Bayonet released on spring

Damascene pattern on barrel

Floral scrollwork on frame

BICYCLE PISTOL

A pistol for use against an annoying yapping dog might seem a bit extreme, but that is the purpose of this French weapon dating to about 1900. It was marketed to cyclists venturing out from their hometowns into rural areas. The idea was that a blank charge would be fired into the face of any dog that seemed aggressive. The pistol could be used to fire real rounds as well.

SINGLE-SHOT POCKET PISTOL

This tiny single-shot percussion-cap pistol has a very small caliber and would not have been able to cope with a powerful charge, so its use against a human assailant might be in question. It was, however, small enough to be tucked into a purse or jacket pocket. The stud trigger became functional only when the hammer was pulled back.

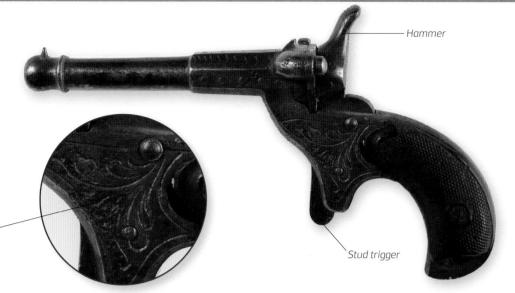

Hammer

Carved-wood decoration

Stud trigger

PATTI PINFIRE REVOLVER

This elegant little pistol in its own wooden box was owned by the famous 19th-century Spanish opera singer Adelina Patti. She first achieved stardom at the age of eight in 1851 and was rarely out of the public eye until her final farewell performance in 1914. Given that she spent her entire adult life cosseted and cared for by a succession of husbands, lovers and business agents, it is difficult to imagine why she needed a gun.

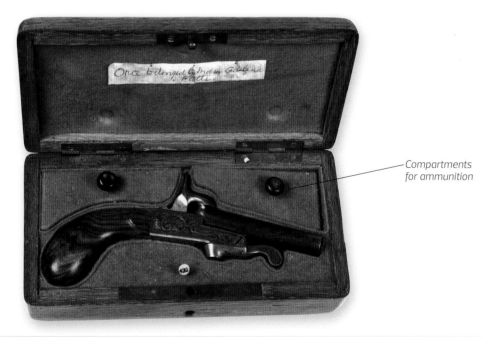

Once belonged to Madam Adelina Patti

Compartments for ammunition

GUN CONTROL

Governments have long sought to control the private ownership of weaponry. In the Roman Empire it was forbidden for non-Roman citizens to own a weapon longer than a few inches, while even citizens needed permission to carry a sword or spear.

In the 21st century, most countries seek to control the ownership of guns in one way or another. Generally a person is required to have a license to own a gun, though the conditions under which a license is issued vary greatly. In Australia a person needs to have a "genuine reason" for needing a gun, and the gun must be suitable for that purpose—hunting, for example. In Britain it is illegal to carry an object made or designed to cause injury in a public place, but not to own one. In China it is almost impossible to obtain a gun license for any reason. In India a license is issued only if a person has credible reason to believe his or her life is in danger. In New Zealand only military-style weapons are controlled; the rest are freely available. It is in the United States, however, where gun control has become a major political issue. The arguments for and against gun control are keenly debated in a way they are not elsewhere.

FOUR-BARRELED POCKET PISTOL

This crude little weapon was made in France in the later 19th century. The harmonica-style quadruple barrel was removed to be loaded, then slid down into the pistol. As each barrel was fired, the pull of the trigger raised the harmonica to bring the next barrel in line with the concealed hammer.

Harmonica-style barrels

Safety catch

SINGLE-SHOT POCKET PISTOL

Fired using a percussion cap, this tiny pistol was designed so that it could be hidden in a sock, glove or other small item of clothing. The trigger remained hidden until the hammer was pulled back, when it then emerged from the case.

Trigger

Hammer

Hammer

Folding trigger

LADY'S MOTHER-OF-PEARL PISTOLS

The mother-of-pearl handles on these two .22 revolvers indicates that they may have been made for a woman. They both have a folding trigger that can be folded flat against the frame when the pistol is not in use.

Mother-of-pearl grips

MUFF GUN

Rather better made than some other pocket pistols, this percussion-cap weapon has an ivory grip and a delicate mechanism. It is therefore thought to have been designed for a woman to carry in her muff.

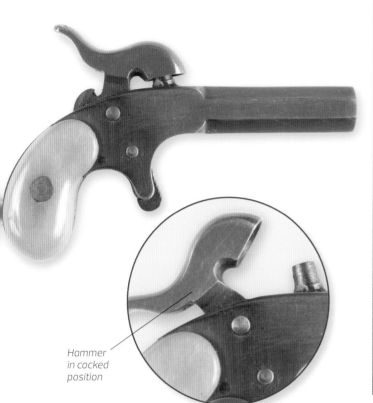

Hammer in cocked position

Introduced in the 16th century, the hand muff was a popular fashion accessory, both beautiful and practical. Common right through to the early 20th century, muffs could conceal a weapon as well as warm the hands.

BELGIAN MUFF PISTOLS

This pair of Belgian-made .36 single-shot percussion pistols is small enough to fit into a muff. Made in the 19th century, the ivory handles show signs of age, but do not detract from the beauty of the weapons.

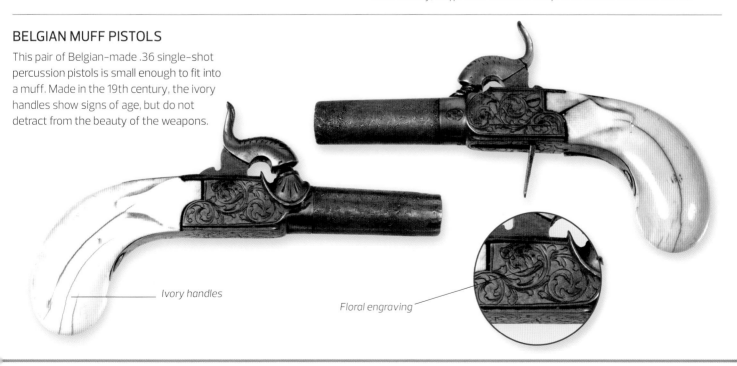

Ivory handles

Floral engraving

BREVETÉ REFORM PISTOLE

Breveté was a small French gunmaker active in the later 19th century manufacturing its own designs and later producing weapons under licenses. Its four barrels that rise with each shot indicates that it was made for personal protection. The safety catch on the left side of the weapon could work loose, making this a potentially hazardous gun to own.

Short 1¼-inch barrels

Gun grip features name of pistol

COLT 1903 POCKET HAMMERLESS

The Colt 1903 Pocket Hammerless was a semiautomatic pistol made by Colt from 1903 to 1945. It holds eight cartridges in the grip magazine, and is capable of holding .32 or .380 cartridges. Famous gangster John Dillinger was carrying one of these in his pocket when FBI agents gunned him down outside a cinema in Chicago in 1934.

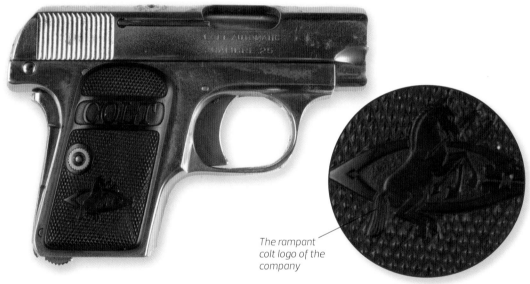

The rampant colt logo of the company

BELGIAN PALM PISTOL

This elegant little weapon is designed to be held in the palm between the thumb and forefinger. It fires .22 ammunition and holds only four cartridges in the cylinder. The design with its folding trigger was well known in Europe, but what makes this example outstanding is the fact that trigger, hammer and rod are made of gold.

Carved-ivory decoration features the pistol's name

FRENCH PALM PISTOL

In the mid-1880s French gunmaker Jacques Rouchouse developed a palm pistol called *Le Merveilleux*—French for "the marvelous." The design was triggerless; to fire, the user squeezed the frame, which activated the side-mounted hammer and discharged a specially made 6mm round. The same system was later used in pistols such as the Gaulois guns.

GAULOIS GUN

The Gaulois family of firearms were made in France in the later 19th century by Manufacture Française d'Armes et Cycles de Saint Etienne. The guns fired a special 8mm Gaulois cartridge. Squeezing the sliding handle moves a cartridge from the magazine in the handle into the barrel and fires it. The safety catch is here in the vertical, or "safe," position. When the catch was turned to the horizontal, the gun was ready to fire. With the catch in the downward position, the slide came out for reloading.

Catch in "safe" position

TRIBUZIO PISTOL

The Italian gunsmith Catello Tribuzio of Turin received a patent for this tiny weapon in 1889. Advertisements described the weapon as being "as flat as a notebook." The weapon was held with the thumb above the safety catch and index finger curled around the front under the barrel. The ring trigger was operated by the middle finger.

PROTECTOR PALM PISTOL

Dubbed "The Protector" by the Parisian gunsmith Jacques Edmond Turbiaux, who invented it in 1882, this odd pistol fired either 6mm or 8mm cartridges. Turbiaux patented the weapon in not only his native France, but also in Britain, Belgium, Italy and the United States, though it is not known how many guns he sold. The cartridges were loaded into the circular magazine facing outward. The weapon was held in the palm and the rear lever squeezed to rotate the magazine, bringing a cartridge in line with the barrel and firing it.

1 ¾-inch half octagonal barrel

Concealed Carry

Owning a weapon comes with certain rules. The legality, or otherwise, for example, of carrying a concealed weapon in public has varied widely over time.

In most countries, a person licensed to own a firearm is not allowed to carry it in a concealed fashion in public. Instead, the gun must be carried in a box or container.

Over the years gunsmiths have made many efforts to get around laws by disguising guns as ordinary objects that are legal to carry in public. Other concealed weapons were, in fact, designed to serve two purposes, such as the walking sticks that hid a gun and were intended for use by gamekeepers in rough territory.

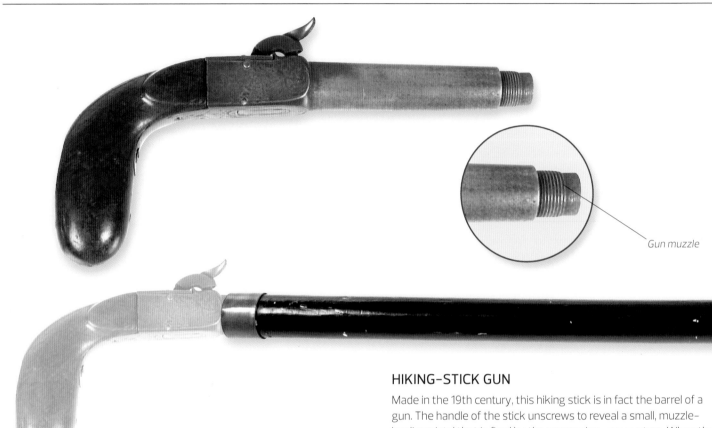

Gun muzzle

HIKING-STICK GUN

Made in the 19th century, this hiking stick is in fact the barrel of a gun. The handle of the stick unscrews to reveal a small, muzzle-loading pistol that is fired by the percussion-cap system. When the hammer is pulled back, the hidden trigger emerges, and the gun is ready to fire at any game animal that comes close enough.

ZIP GUNS

Strictly speaking, a "zip gun" is a firearm manufactured by a person other than a trained gunsmith. In common usage, however, the term has come to apply to homemade weapons, usually produced for or by criminals, which disguise an often-crude gun as a legal object. This tiny gun is made of a steel tube with a concealed spring that fires the cartridge. It dates from the Cold War era just after World War II.

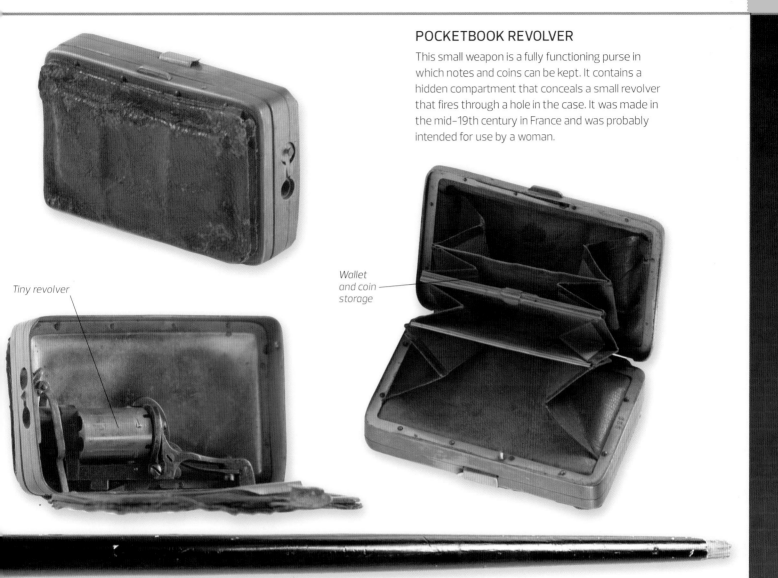

POCKETBOOK REVOLVER

This small weapon is a fully functioning purse in which notes and coins can be kept. It contains a hidden compartment that conceals a small revolver that fires through a hole in the case. It was made in the mid-19th century in France and was probably intended for use by a woman.

Wallet and coin storage

Tiny revolver

AMERICAN MACHINE-GUN SHELL

When it is closed, this appears to be a .50 caliber machine-gun cartridge of the type used by machine guns on American bombers during World War II. Air gunners frequently carried such cartridges, often for luck, so this would attract little attention. When unclipped, it reveals a small .22 spring-loaded gun.

Combination Weapons

While concealed weapons seek to hide a gun inside an innocuous object with the intention of disguising it from passersby or law enforcement officials, a combination weapon is one that combines two different weapons into one object. In many cases there is no intention to deceive anyone, and both weapons are in full view.

The motivation here was usually that early firearms were not always reliable, or they discharged only one shot and could leave their user unarmed when faced by more than one opponent. Other combination weapons did have the aim of deceiving an enemy, luring them forward in the expectation that they faced only one type of weapon until the other was revealed. These combinations have nearly always been personal purchases by individuals, and even when used in a military setting, they have not been part of the official armaments handed out by armies.

TURKISH GUN–SHIELD

Measuring 16 inches across, this bronze shield was made in Turkey. These bucklers were used by men armed with swords. Their small size and light weight enabled the swordsman to adopt a fast-moving, athletic style of combat. This example, however, has a gun hidden behind it that fires forward. The gun was fired by a string that was attached to the user's belt so that the gun went off when the shield was pushed forward. It was probably intended to lure an opponent forward under the impression that he faced a man armed only with a sword and buckler, whereupon he would be shot.

ETHIOPIAN GUN–SHIELD

Ethiopian shields were made in highly decorated forms. The vast majority were made of hippopotamus hide that was soaked in hot water and then stretched over a wooden mold to create an embossed pattern that was then painted. Noblemen, however, decorated the fronts of their shields with pierced metal work that would be polished to reflect the sun. This example has a gun barrel protruding from its center to be discharged at an enemy.

Gun barrel

INDIAN PISTOL-SHIELD

Made in the first half of the 19th century, this Indian metal shield is of a style known as a Mughal dhal. The four metal bosses on the face hid the fixings for leather straps behind, which allowed the shield to be held in one hand. A pierced metal shield of this type would usually have been backed by tough leather. In this example, however, the bosses have a more deadly purpose—behind each is a flintlock pistol pointing directly forward, ready to be fired at the unwary.

One of four muzzles

Phoenix-head club

EUROPEAN CLUB-GUN

This ornamental weapon from Europe dates to the early 19th century. The gun barrel to the right is fairly obvious, while the heavy, animal head to the left can clearly be used as a club once the gun has been fired. There is also a hidden knife blade.

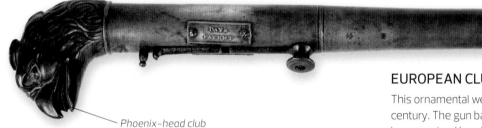

INDIAN MACE-PISTOL

This steel mace was made in India, perhaps in the 17th century. It was adapted in the 19th century to have a percussion-cap pistol attached to it.

Exposed percussion-cap mechanism

TRUNCHEON GUN

In 19th century Britain, the truncheon was a wooden club about 12 to 18 inches long that was carved from a single piece of hardwood such as oak or mahogany. Traditionally they were the only weapon carried by policemen on duty and were designed to give the police a crucial advantage in the types of scuffles then common on the streets. This example has been adapted in an unofficial way to include a percussion-cap pistol at its end.

POCKETKNIFE PERCUSSION PISTOLS

Knives with blades that fold into a wooden handle have been made since Roman times, but it was not until the mid-19th century that pocketknives containing more than one blade, along with screwdrivers, nail clippers and other tools began appearing. These examples include a small pistol which is cocked when the concealed trigger is pulled out ready for firing.

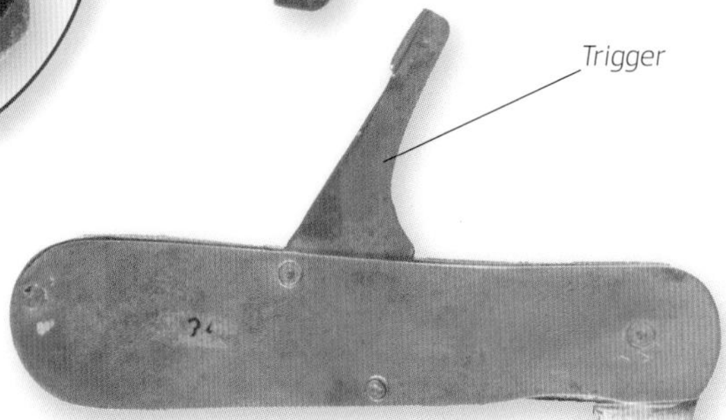

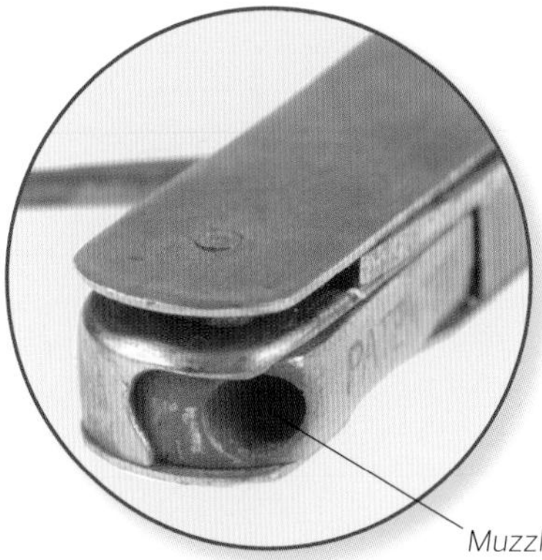

Muzzle

Trigger

Folding blades

Muzzle

DIRK-PISTOL

During the later 18th and early 19th centuries, naval battles were sometimes decided by boarding parties: men from one ship storming aboard another to overpower the crew and force the captain to surrender. In the closely confined spaces of a ship's deck, the fighters would use pistols and short-bladed swords known as cutlasses. This weapon, made by French company Dumonthier & Sons in the 1840s, combined a twin-barrelled percussion-cap pistol with a blade similar to that of a bowie knife. The French navy fought few actions at this time, so it is unlikely this weapon saw any use.

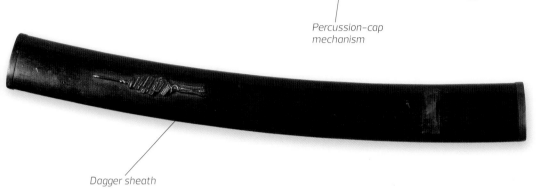

Percussion-cap mechanism

Dagger sheath

JAPANESE DAGGER-PISTOL

This Japanese weapon from the later 19th century looks like a traditional *wakizashi*, or samurai short sword. The wakizashi was traditionally worn tucked into a waist sash alongside the katana, or long sword, with the pairing being the traditional sign that the owner was a samurai, not just a soldier. This *wakizashi*, however, is a percussion-cap pistol that would have given its user a concealed advantage no true samurai would have considered using.

FRENCH KNIFE-PISTOL

This high-quality weapon was made in France in the late 19th century. The ivory handle of the tempered-steel dagger conceals a single-shot gun taking a .32 centerfire metal cartridge. The trigger appears only when the hammer is pulled back.

Carved ivory decorates the frame and grip

CUTLASS-PISTOL

Pistol barrel

This .31 caliber percussion-cap pistol can only fire a single shot before it needs to be reloaded. It does, however, have a cutlass blade attached to it in case the user is attacked while reloading. The handle is clearly designed to be used with the pistol and would have been unwieldy when using the cutlass, so this must be considered something of an emergency weapon.

COMBO PISTOL-DAGGER

This vicious weapon appears at first glance to be a percussion-cap, single-shot pistol with an impressively wide caliber of .80 inch. In fact, it conceals two edged weapons. There is a 6½-inch straight blade that slides forward from under the barrel to appear like a bayonet. There is also an 8-inch curved blade secreted in the handle that can be flicked out to be held in place by a spring.

Trigger guard doubles as a hilt

Revolver cylinder

APACHE PISTOL

During the final quarter of the 19th century, Paris was plagued by gangs of tough young criminals who mugged passersby, stole whatever they could grab and fought murderous feuds with one another and the police. The gangs adopted a distinctive style of dress that included flared trousers, loose-fitting shirts, neck scarves, peaked caps and pointed, brightly colored shoes. The press dubbed the gangs "Apache," comparing their savagery with the stereotypes of the Apache tribe from the United States. In time, the Apache style of dress became fashionable among French youth seeking a rebellious look. and all sorts of objects were termed "Apache" in an effort to give them a flavor of youthful rebellion. The gunsmiths of Liege produced this murderous looking weapon that combines knuckleduster, pistol and dagger and called it an "Apache pistol," though its link to the Parisian street gangs is dubious.

AMERICAN PISTOL-KNIFE

This tiny object combines a short dagger blade with a small-caliber single-shot gun. It was made in the United States in the later 19th century.

LE CENTENAIRE

Known in France as a *coup-de-poing* or "kick-fist," this nasty weapon is a knuckleduster with a small percussion-cap single-shot gun hidden in its handle. This example was made in France in 1889.

FLINTLOCK PISTOL-AXE

This flintlock pistol was made in France in the late 18th century. It has a small axe head attached to its muzzle. Traditionally this pistol was thought to have been a naval weapon, used when the crew of one warship boarded another. There are no contemporary records of this weapon being used in naval battles, so its true purpose remains a mystery.

Flintlock mechanism

Axe

KNIFE-REVOLVER

This crudely made combination weapon has a six-shot revolver merged into a folding pocketknife. The poor quality construction indicates that it was made in a back street workshop for a single customer.

Revolver cylinder

Folding trigger

SPANISH DAGGER-PISTOL

This Spanish weapon dates to the middle of the 19th century. It is a well-made, single-shot percussion-cap pistol. When the trigger guard is pulled back, the short bayonet flips forward and locks into place.

Bayonet blade

The World at War

Modern Warfare

Warfare changed dramatically in the 20th century. In 1900, cavalrymen riding horses and wielding lances or sabers alongside their carbines were a familiar sight on maneuvers and in army camps. By 2000, horses had vanished entirely, to be replaced by tanks and armored personnel carriers, while aircraft roared overhead and guided missiles hit distant targets with unerring accuracy.

Although so much changed in the military world, much remained the same. All the sophisticated machinery in the world could not replace "boots on the ground" when it came to occupying, pacifying and securing an area.

Infantry remain infantry, and the weapons they use perform much the same function today as they did a century ago. That is not to say that they have remained the same. There have been important technological changes.

BATTLE OF BROODSEINDE
(PASSCHENDAELE/WORLD WAR I)
Men of the 8th Battalion, East Yorkshire Regiment going up to the line near Frezenberg.

Handguns of World War I

All the armies that went to war in 1914 expected the war to be fought in much the same way that the American Civil War or Franco–Prussian War had been fought. Large armies would march across Europe, seeking positions of advantage on hills or behind rivers from which to defeat their enemies in massed battles of envelopment, movement and withdrawals.

The tasks of an officer in such battles were primarily to maintain discipline among his men, watch for movements of enemy formations and to lead his men into battle. He did not need to be encumbered with a rifle, nor did his job involve actually shooting at the enemy at long range. He needed a weapon for personal protection in close combat. Some officers and armies still favored the sword, but by 1914 the pistol was the usual sidearm for an officer.

Building on the experiences of the Franco–Prussian War, most armies had adopted a revolver as their standard pistol. The reasons for this were that revolvers had a proven track record of reliability in tough campaigning conditions, were easy to maintain and were cheap to buy. The sudden emergence of static trench warfare would soon impact on the choice of sidearm, as it did on so much else.

Ring attached to trooper's clothing via lanyard

GERMAN REVOLVER

In 1908 the German army officially adopted the Luger P08 to be its officer pistol of choice. Still, many officers viewed the semiautomatic action with suspicion and preferred to trust their lives to a tried-and-tested revolver action. Many simply kept their old M1883 revolvers, a single-action, .44 six-shot revolver. Others purchased their own guns. This six-shot pistol, which is chambered for the German army's .44 cartridge, is a civilian weapon adapted to military use by the addition of a lanyard ring.

STEYR M1912

The Steyr M1912 was the standard issue sidearm to officers in the Austro-Hungarian army in World War I. It was based on an earlier design for a semiautomatic pistol, the M1907, upgraded for military use. The German army bought about 10,000 of these pistols during World War I. After peace came in 1918, the pistol continued to be produced for the civilian market, mostly sold to the export trade. The military version returned to production in 1938 with 50,000 being acquired by the German army after the annexation of Austria.

Slide moves back to load cartridges

.455 caliber,
six-shot cylinder

CONTRACT COLT NEW SERVICE REVOLVER

Designed by Colt in 1898, the New Service Revolver was adopted by the U.S. Army in 1909 as the M1909. The military pistol was chambered to take the .45 Colt cartridge as this was deemed to have the stopping power to knock down even the most determined enemy at close range. The pistol was later sold to the Canadian army and, when chambered to take the .455 Webley cartridge, to the British army. The gun remained in production after the war and around 360,000 were built in all.

As men headed off to the front to fight the war, women headed to the factories to supply them with the weaponry. Above are female munitions workers grinding barrels of automatic .45s, in Colt's Patent Firearms Manufacturing Company, Hartford, Connecticut, c. 1914–18.

GLISENTI 1884 REVOLVER

The Italian arms company Società Siderurgica Glisenti was only one of many small Italian arms companies that operated on a workshop basis. The companies would cooperate on production if one weapon achieved large orders that its designer could not meet. As a consequence, manufacturing standards varied somewhat, a problem the would bedevil the Italian arms industry well into the 20th century. This revolver design was produced by Glisenti in 1884 with a folding trigger than came down when the hammer was cocked. It was also produced with a fixed trigger and trigger guard.

Folding trigger

GLISENTI M1910 AUTO

This example of the popular Glisenti M1910 is shown with its recoil slide pulled back. When the gun is fired, the barrel and bolt slide back together. The barrel then stops as the used cartridge is expelled, with the block disengaging from the barrel to strip the new cartridge from the magazine. The block then reengages the barrel and moves back to the firing position, whereupon a wedge rises from the frame to lock everything into position. This action was smooth and efficient, but proved to be rather fragile on campaign and led to the pistol jamming rather more than was healthy for those who used it.

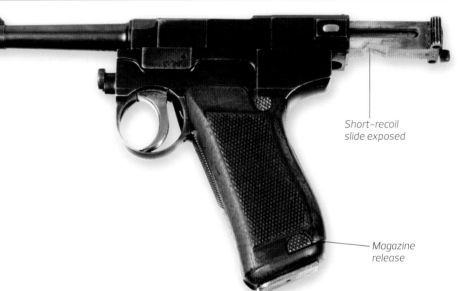

Short-recoil slide exposed

Magazine release

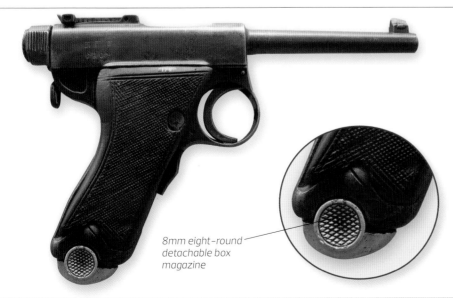

8mm eight-round detachable box magazine

SECOND MODEL NAMBU PISTOL

In 1902 Lieutenant General Kijiru Nambu of the Imperial Japanese Army produced a design for a semiautomatic 8mm pistol. The army did not adopt the design itself, but did make small numbers for sale to private individuals. In 1907 Nambu produced a lighter version to fire 7mm ammunition, and this again achieved good private sales but no official orders. In 1909 the Japanese navy bought large numbers of the 8mm version, shown here, for use by landing parties and marine officers, and the Thai army later placed large orders. In 1924 Nambu introduced a new variant, the Type 14, which saw extensive service with Japanese forces in World War II.

BERGMANN–BAYARD M1910

This M1910 version of the Bergmann–Bayard pistol was manufactured in Belgium for use by the Danish navy. It fired 9mm ammunition from a 6- or 10-round magazine located in front of the trigger. The earlier M1908 version had been sold to the Spanish military in large numbers. In August 1914 the invading German armies laid siege to Liege, pounding much of the city to rubble with massive 42cm siege howitzers. The Bergmann–Bayard factory was first damaged, then captured. Cut off from supplies from Belgium, the Spanish Largo company began producing Bergmann ammunition, which is now known widely as the 9mm Largo.

Detachable 7.65mm magazine

SERGEANT YORK

Sergeant Alvin York was one of the most decorated of U.S. soldiers in World War I. He is certainly the best known, largely thanks to *Sergeant York*, a 1941 movie about his exploits that starred Gary Cooper as York. Ironically, York applied for the status of conscientious objector because he attended the Church of Christ in Christian Union, which opposed all violence. The appeal was turned down, and York was persuaded of the rightness of fighting by his company commander.

On October 8, 1918, York's unit was advancing near Decauville when it was pinned down by German machine-gun fire. York and seven men were sent to outflank the machine-gun nest and destroy it. As they worked their way forward, York and his men discovered a German command post, capturing all the men in it. Leaving his men to guard the prisoners, York pushed on alone.

As he approached a knoll from which he would get a shot at the machine-gun nest, York was suddenly attacked by six Germans, who leaped out of a hidden trench and charged him with fixed bayonets. York pulled out his Colt .45 and shot all six before they reached him. A German officer then appeared and surrendered. York accepted, not realizing that the German was actually surrendering his entire company. A few minutes later York marched 132 German prisoners back to his astonished company commander. It was for this action that York was awarded the Medal of Honor.

L'EXPLORATEUR MITRAILLE

This unusual double-barreled revolver was chambered to take 6mm ammunition, with 12 cartridges in the cylinder, two of which were fired at a time. It was marketed by the Manufacture Française d'Armes et Cycles de St. Etienne, a specialist mail-order company based in the French industrial city of St. Etienne. The guns were manufactured by a number of small companies, and most were sold to the colonial market, hence its name of "Explorer."

Cylinder takes 12 rounds

EUROPEAN SIX-SHOT REVOLVER

This early-20th-century revolver has a sliding rod on its side that can be pushed back to eject cartridges from the cylinder. The addition of a lanyard to the base of the grip indicates that it has been adapted for military use.

Sliding ramrod

SCHEINTOD HAHN GAS REVOLVER

Scheintod is German for "almost dead" and indicates that this pistol was designed to shoot tear-gas canisters produced in .44 caliber pistol ammunition. The weapon was generally a piece of police equipment, but when used to fire shotgun cartridges could be used as a murderous short-range weapon by officers engaged in trench fighting.

Grip features a dancing skeleton

Folding trigger without a safety guard

GERMAN ARMY REVOLVER

This German revolver was manufactured in Erfurt, the capital of the province of Thuringia, in 1893. It is chambered to take .44 ammunition and has a single action. At this time, Erfurt was a heavily industrialized town filled with small workshops that specialized in producing almost any sort of mechanical device a customer wanted. This weapon appears to have been a one-off product.

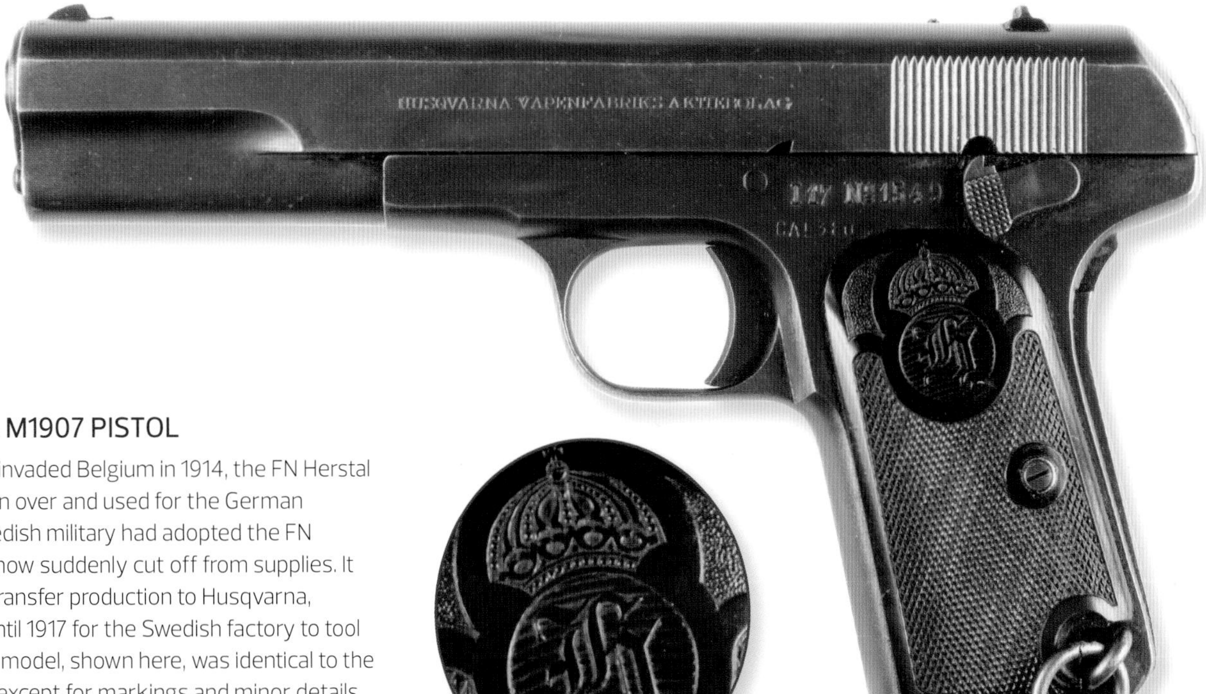

Lanyard ring

Wooden grip

HUSQVARNA M1907 PISTOL

When Germany invaded Belgium in 1914, the FN Herstal factory was taken over and used for the German military. The Swedish military had adopted the FN M1907 and was now suddenly cut off from supplies. It was decided to transfer production to Husqvarna, though it took until 1917 for the Swedish factory to tool up. The Swedish model, shown here, was identical to the Belgian original, except for markings and minor details. It remained in production until 1941, after which spare parts remained available to 2000.

Husqvarna logo

FN Herstal
logo on grip

Lanyard hook

Doughboy with pistol belt, M1917 revolver in holster
and the revolver ammunition pocket

BROWNING PATENT PISTOL

The M1910 semiautomatic pistol was designed by John Browning for FN Herstal in Belgium. The prototype for this model was completed in 1908 and patented on February 20, 1909. The factory was ready to begin production some six months later, but manufacturing was halted because sales of the M1900 were still high, and the factory wanted to maximize profits. By the time the M1910 was released for sale it was 1912, so the model name was changed to "New Model Browning," the official M1910 designation not being used until the 1920s.

CHINESE SEMIAUTOMATIC PISTOL

The Chinese Empire was under severe strain in the early years of the 20th century. Economic decline was serious and several provincial governors were seeking to achieve near independence from the central government. In such conditions, it was impossible for foreign companies to enforce patents on Chinese industry, and copies of foreign products became common. This 7.63mm semiautomatic is an almost direct copy of Mauser weapons.

Ribbed grip

Gangster Warfare

Bandits, robbers and outlaws have used violence to get their hands on valuables since the dawn of time. When firearms became available, criminals quickly adopted them for nefarious purposes. Still, the criminal lifestyle makes specific demands on the firearms that a crook uses. Generally a criminal will want to have a gun that can be easily concealed, works reliably and does not require much care or maintenance. During the 1920s and 1930s, the United States had a particular problem with large-scale, organized gangs of criminals who imported or manufactured alcoholic drinks, then banned in the United States under Prohibition. These gangs made vast amounts of money, some of which was used to bribe policemen and politicians to look the other way. The gangs fought frequently murderous wars to control territory and trades. Very often the weapons used by and against the gangsters were surplus military guns left over from World War I.

LILLIPUT PISTOL

Designed for personal protection, the Lilliput pistol was named after the fictional island of Lilliput in *Gulliver's Travels*, where people were only about six inches tall. The gun was made in Suhl, Germany, from 1920 to 1929 and lived up to its name by being only 4 inches long and firing 4.25mm cartridges. It is believed that the notorious female bandit Bonnie Parker (of Bonnie and Clyde fame) kept a Lilliput pistol on her at all times, though in photos of her she is shown posing with a larger pistol.

4-inch long pistol

Leather pistol case to hold gun and cartridge tray

Bonnie Parker posing with pistol and cigar

COLT POLICE POSITIVE

The Colt Police Positive, shown here in its medium-barrel-length variant, was launched in 1907 with the express aim of equipping policemen with a robust, reliable revolver. This is an early model with the black rubber grip, models made after 1923 having a checkered walnut grip and a heavier frame. The model achieved better accuracy by having a tight fit between the cylinder and the barrel. It remained in production until 1947.

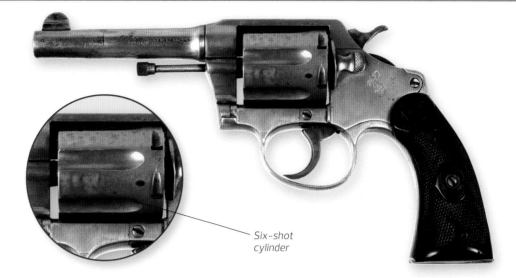

Six-shot cylinder

John Dillinger

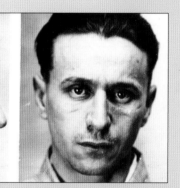

Fred Barker

"Pretty Boy" Floyd

Al Capone

GANGSTERS AND GUNS: WEAPONS IN THE WRONG HANDS

Shown here are four of the most wanted U.S. gangsters of the 1920s and 1930s.

John Dillinger robbed 24 banks, held up dozens of shops and other establishments and escaped from prison twice. In one of his prison breaks, Dillinger produced a .38 Colt pistol to overpower the guards. Although he was known to favor this pistol, this particular gun turned out to be an exact replica Dillinger had whittled from wood in his cell.

Fred Barker was the second of five boys born to "Ma" Barker, who organized her boys into a highly successful criminal gang. In his fatal shootout with police in January 1935, he used a Tommy gun submachine gun.

Charles Floyd, who was known for robbing banks, earned his nickname of "Pretty Boy" from a wanted notice in 1925 that described him as "young and pretty." in his final shootout, Floyd used a Colt .45 pistol.

Notorious Chicago gangster Al Capone is known to have murdered several men with a pistol and the Tommy gun, but he was eventually convicted of tax evasion and died at home of a heart attack in 1947.

Axis Pistols of World War II

World War II was fought between two great alliances, neither of which had much in common with each other apart from their choice of enemies. The Axis alliance began in 1936, when Germany and Japan signed the Anti-Comintern Pact aimed against Russia, which both recognized as an opponent of their territorial ambitions. In 1939 Italy agreed to a military alliance with Germany, completing the three main powers in the Axis. In 1941

Romania joined Germany in the invasion of Russia to regain lands lost to Russia some years earlier. Finland also joined the war on Russia to regain lost territory. Bulgaria helped the Germans occupy Yugoslavia, but declared it was not part of the Axis. Thailand lent important support to Japan in Southeast Asia, though without a formal alliance. Iraq is sometimes considered an Axis power, as it fought a short war against Britain in 1941.

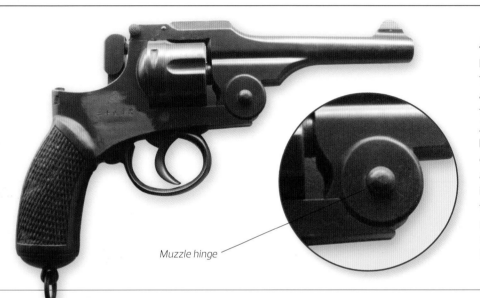

Muzzle hinge

JAPANESE TYPE 26 REVOLVER

Entering service with the Japanese army in 1893, the Type 36 revolver fired 9mm ammunition from a 6-round cylinder. This was the first pistol made in Japan to be used by the Japanese armed forces, earlier guns having been imported from the United States. It was designed and made at the Koishikawa Arsenal, and while the design process was kept secret, it is thought the Japanese copied elements from a variety of imported weapons to produce this gun. Although it was officially replaced by later models, the Type 26 was still in use with some officers in 1945.

Raised sights

Scale and cursor sights

ARTILLERY LUGER

Although the standard carbine version of the Luger P08 semiautomatic pistol came with an 8-inch barrel, a few were manufactured with this impressive 12-inch barrel. This version, which came complete with a wooden shoulder stock that doubled as a holster, was sold to civilians for hunting and was not intended for military use.

ASTRA 600 PISTOL

The Astra 600 was a rugged semiautomatic that fired 9mm cartridges from an 8-round box magazine in the grip. The guns were commissioned from Spain by Germany as an alternative to the Luger. Around 11,000 were delivered between summer 1943 and summer 1944, when the Allied liberation of France blocked exports to Germany. The pistol remained in production to 1945, with many of the later examples going to police use.

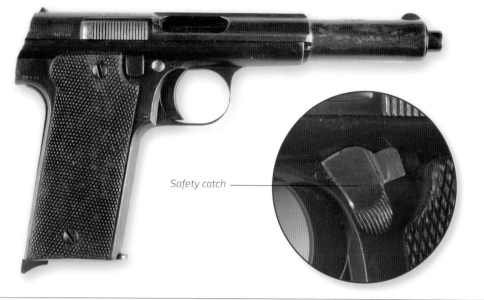

Safety catch

Jointed arm in closed position

Trommelmagazin 08

LUGER WITH DRUM MAGAZINE

An optional accessory for the German Luger was the 32-round drum magazine known as the Trommelmagazin 08. Officially the drum magazine was available for private purchasers and was intended for use hunting or target shooting. Some officers chose, however to purchase one to take to war. This example was taken from a staff officer of the Afrika Korps when that army surrendered in Tunis in May 1943.

WALTHER ARMS

Since 1886 the name *Walther* has been associated with technological breakthroughs in the design of small arms, a reputation the company upholds to this day. The business was founded in the small town of Zella-Mehils, tucked away deep in the forests of Thuringia in southern Germany, by gunsmith Carl Walther who had earlier worked for Mauser.

At first the company made high-quality hunting rifles, but in 1908 Carl's son Fritz took over the company and decided to try making a pistol. His first design was not a success and is a now a very rare collector's item.

In 1929 Fritz Walther produced his first PP model, short for "Police Pistol." In 1931 the first PPK ("Police Pistol Short") followed with the first widespread use of stamped metal parts to keep costs down. After the factory was destroyed in World War II, the company moved to Ulm, where it remains to this day.

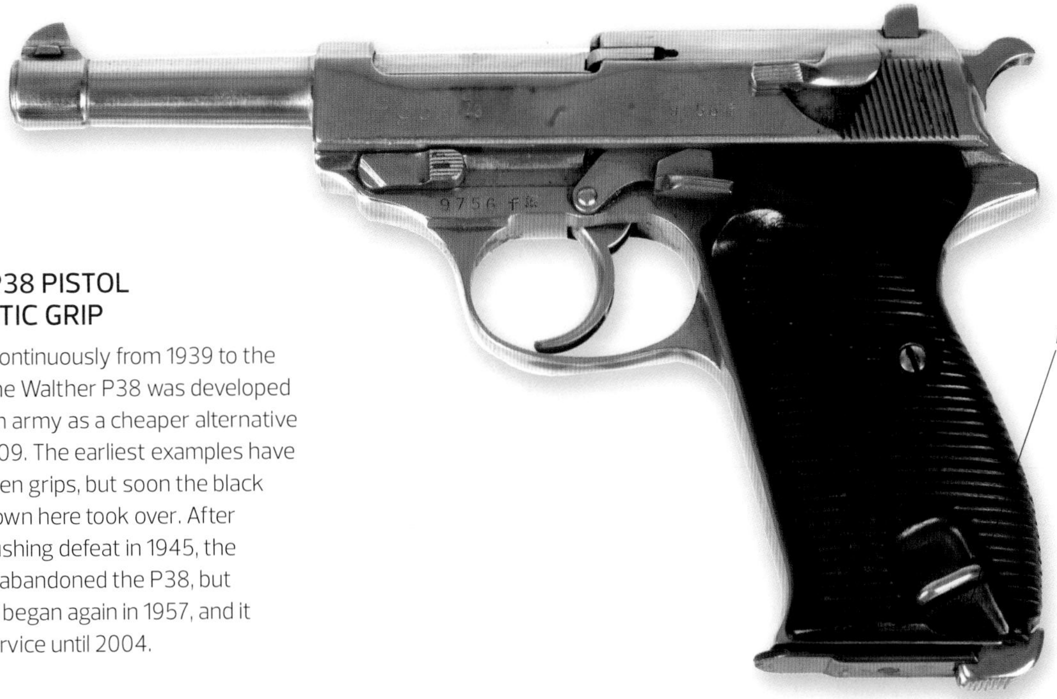

WALTHER P38 PISTOL WITH PLASTIC GRIP

In production continuously from 1939 to the present day, the Walther P38 was developed for the German army as a cheaper alternative to the Luger P09. The earliest examples have polished wooden grips, but soon the black plastic grip shown here took over. After Germany's crushing defeat in 1945, the German army abandoned the P38, but military orders began again in 1957, and it remained in service until 2004.

Magazine release

WALTHER P38 PISTOL WITH WOODEN GRIP

This early version of the P38 has the original wooden grip and has seen some hard use, probably as a sidearm in World War II. The very first examples of the P38 had an internal hammer, but the German army soon insisted on an external hammer, as seen here. Mass production began in 1940, with an 8-round magazine in the grip and using the 9 x 19mm parabellum cartridge, also used in the Luger pistol.

5-inch barrel

Soviet and U.S. officers near Elbe River, Germany, on April 28, 1945. At left a Soviet officer's TT33 lies before him in the grass; at center a Soviet captain's Luger is tucked into his belt; and at right, reclining, a U.S. lieutenant wears a holstered Colt 1911 and holds in his had Walther P38 captured from a German soldier.

Magazine release

BERETTA M1934

The Beretta M1934 was designed and produced exclusively for the Italian armed forces from 1937 to 1945 and remained in production to 1991. Designed to be used in a range of environments from North African deserts to Alpine snows, the M1934 has a very tough construction and is easy to maintain with a minimum of tools. Beretta boasts that it has a working life of 100 years.

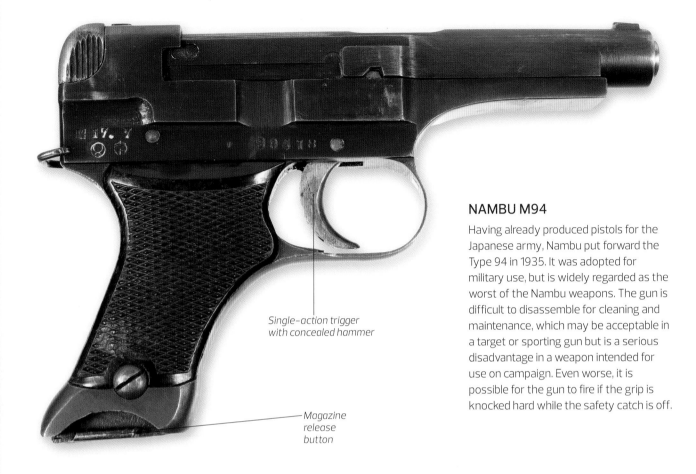

Single-action trigger with concealed hammer

Magazine release button

NAMBU M94

Having already produced pistols for the Japanese army, Nambu put forward the Type 94 in 1935. It was adopted for military use, but is widely regarded as the worst of the Nambu weapons. The gun is difficult to disassemble for cleaning and maintenance, which may be acceptable in a target or sporting gun but is a serious disadvantage in a weapon intended for use on campaign. Even worse, it is possible for the gun to fire if the grip is knocked hard while the safety catch is off.

THE DESERT FOX

German Field Marshal Erwin Rommel is best known as a highly skilled Panzer commander who brought humanity and professionalism, and at times a sense of humor, to his conduct of war. Military historians tend to study his part in the 1940 invasion of France, when he commanded the Seventh Panzer Division, and more particularly his years in command of the fabled Afrika Korps in North Africa, where he earned his nickname of "Desert Fox."

Rommel first went to war armed not with a tank but a Luger pistol. On August 22, 1914, he was scouting ahead of his 124th Wurttemburg Regiment with three men when he came across a farmhouse manned by 20 French soldiers. Rather than wait for his platoon to come up, Rommel led a dash to the farmhouse, having first armed his men with bundles of burning straw. These were pushed through the open windows, followed by shots and loud shouts. The French fled, and Rommel had gained his first victory.

In October 1917 Rommel was on the Italian Front and in command of a battalion of infantry. During the Austro–German offensive at Monte Matajur, Rommel saw to his front what appeared to be an unguarded ravine. Leading his 600 men in single file, Rommel eventually found himself right behind the Italian lines. He marched into a rest camp, drew his men up with leveled rifles and ordered 3,500 Italians to surrender, which they did. He then positioned his troops to block the retreat route of the Italians at the front, and over the next 48 hours captured another 6,000 men and 81 guns. He was awarded Germany's highest decoration, the Pour le Merité.

NAMBU M14

The Nambu M14 was a development of earlier Nambu pistols. Production of it began in 1925, and it was officially adopted for Japanese officers in 1927. Officers soon reported that the trigger guard was too small to allow them to insert their fingers when wearing gloves in cold weather, so later models had a larger trigger guard, as on this example. After 1942, wartime shortages led to a minor redesign to make production easier, but it reduced quality, and cartridge jams became more common.

Enlarged trigger guard

Detachable box magazine

Muzzle is hinged

Slide is removable

CZECH CZ VZ38 PISTOL

In the 1930s the Czechoslovak armed forces commissioned arms manufacturer Česká zbrojovka Strakonice to produce a pistol to replace the aging weapons inherited from the old Austro-Hungarian Empire. The result was the VZ38, a solid semiautomatic with a 9-round magazine. Before production could begin the Czech lands were invaded by Germany, so the entire production run went to arm the German army.

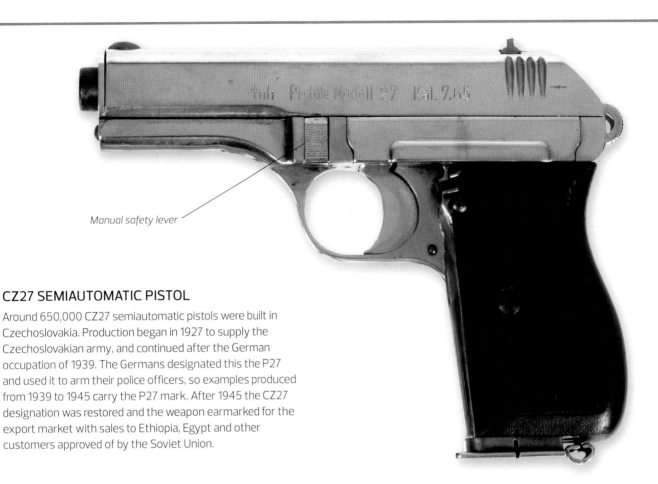

Manual safety lever

CZ27 SEMIAUTOMATIC PISTOL

Around 650,000 CZ27 semiautomatic pistols were built in Czechoslovakia. Production began in 1927 to supply the Czechoslovakian army, and continued after the German occupation of 1939. The Germans designated this the P27 and used it to arm their police officers, so examples produced from 1939 to 1945 carry the P27 mark. After 1945 the CZ27 designation was restored and the weapon earmarked for the export market with sales to Ethiopia, Egypt and other customers approved of by the Soviet Union.

HITLER'S SUICIDE

Dictator of Germany from 1934, Adolf Hitler led Germany to vast conquests between 1939 and 1942. Yet, by April 1945 Germany stood poised on the brink of utter defeat and Russian armies were entering the suburbs of Berlin. Hitler retreated to an underground bunker with his most loyal staff while the fighting raged through the city. On April 28 he learned that his previously loyal lieutenants Hermann Göring and Heinrich Himmler had abandoned him, and next day that Italian dictator Benito Mussolini had been captured and then shot by partisans. On April 30 the news was broken that the defenders of Berlin had less than 24 hours of ammunition left. Surrender was inevitable. At 2:30 p.m. Hitler and his long-term girlfriend, now wife, Eva Braun, retired to their bedroom. An hour later a shot was heard. Hitler's valet entered to find Braun dead from cyanide poisoning and Hitler dead from a self-inflicted gunshot wound to the head. The shot had been fired with a Walther PPK semiautomatic pistol.

Eva Braun and Hitler with their dogs at Obersalzberg, Bavaria, in June 1942

Allied Pistols of World War II

The first of the countries that would later make up the Allies was China, which had been invaded by Japan in 1937. When Germany invaded Poland in 1939, Polish allies France and Britain joined the war. Poland surrendered in 1939 and France in 1940. Within weeks, the British Commonwealth countries of Canada, Australia, New Zealand, India, South Africa and various colonies had also joined on the side of Britain. By that date Germany had also invaded and crushed Denmark, Norway, Holland, Belgium and Luxembourg. The Soviet Union joined in 1941 when attacked by Germany, and the United States later that year after the Japanese attack on Pearl Harbor. Thereafter numerous other countries joined the Allies for various reasons: Brazil when German U-boats sank Brazilian merchant ships, Mongolia when told to do so by Russia and Chile as the war drew to its close.

Magazine release

SWEDISH M40 PISTOL

When Germany went to war in 1939 the government stopped all exports of munitions because everything would be needed by the German armed forces. That left the Swedish army in a quandary—it had just chosen a Walther design to reequip its officers. The Swedes then turned to Finland and acquired the right to manufacture the L35 pistol. The Swedish model was dubbed the M40 and incorporated changes to make it cheaper to manufacture. Not realized at the time was the fact that these changes weakened the bolts. The weakness became clear 30 years later when pistols began to explode or fracture, and the model was then removed from service.

Removable side plate

CZECH CZ VZ45 PISTOL

In 1945 Czechoslovakia had been liberated from Germany and was enjoying a brief existence as a relatively free country before it had a Communist government imposed on it by the Soviet Union. During that interlude the CZ45 was designed as a simplified version of the pre-war CZ36. It fires .25 ACP ammunition from an 8-round magazine.

TOKAREV TT33

In 1930 the Red Army decided that the Soviet Union needed to replace the pistols it had been using since the days of the Tsar. Coincidentally, Fedor Tokarev had been designing a pistol based on the Browning M1911. Dubbing this the TT30, the Red Army ordered it to go into production. Almost at once Tokarev introduced changes to the barrel, frame and trigger to make the weapon quicker and cheaper to manufacture. This redesign became the TT33 shown here. It became the standard sidearm for Red Army officers and remains in production to this day, with about 1.7 million having been built.

Soviet lieutenant waving a TT33 pistol, Ukraine, 1942

Spurless hammer

ENFIELD NO. 2 MARK 1* REVOLVER

The Enfield No. 2 Mark 1* was designed in the 1930s as a version of the Enfield No. 2 that had been produced in the 1920s. It was designed to be used by tank crews and had features to adapt it to use in confined spaces. The hammer lacked a spur so it did not snag on controls or clothing, which meant that the gun had to be a double-action pistol.

Spurless hammer

SHORT-BARRELED ENFIELD NO. 2 MARK 1* REVOLVER

In 1942 this version of the Enfield No. 2 Mark 1* appeared with an even shorter barrel. It was for use by commandos and other specialist troops who needed a small weapon to keep in their webbing. Only a small number were produced. As might be expected with such a short barrel, it was effective only at very short range.

Spurless hammer

Plastic grip

ENFIELD NO. 2 MKII REVOLVER

The Enfield revolver proved to be a very durable design. It began life in 1880 as a pistol designed for use by the Royal Northwest Mounted Police—the famous Canadian Mounties—in the days when they still wore their iconic red tunics. It was later adopted by the British army, but it was found that it became inaccurate with wear. In the 1920s the gun was redesigned to become the Enfield No. 2, which fired .380 ammunition from a 6-round cylinder. In this guise it remained in production to 1957.

GENERAL PATTON

George Patton was born into a Virginia family that had provided soldiers to the U.S. Army for generations. He joined the army as a cavalryman, designing a new saber, but soon moved to armored vehicles. He became a passionate advocate of the importance of tanks in modern warfare, and by the time the United States joined World War II he was a general in command of the Second Armored Division. He first entered combat in North Africa during Operation Torch and commanded the Seventh Army with great success during the invasion of Sicily.

Having established a reputation as the most daring and aggressive of Allied commanders, Patton was given the Third Army for the invasion of France in 1944. His armored drive across France was massively successful, and in 1945 he led his army into Germany itself. Throughout the war Patton wore a pistol with an ivory handle and became known in the press as "Two-Gun Patton." In fact Patton did have two ivory-handled pistols, but they were not a matching pair, and he did not wear them together. One was a .45 Colt; the other was a .357 Smith & Wesson. There is only one known photo of him wearing both, and that was staged for the press.

WEBLEY & SCOTT

Webley & Scott is one of Britain's oldest firearms companies. The company traces its history back to the early 18th century, when Birmingham smith William Davies began making bullet molds to go with flintlock pistols and muskets being made by gunsmiths in the city. In 1834 the business passed to Philip Webley, who had married into the Davies family, and he began producing percussion-cap shotguns and rifles. In 1897 the company merged with W & C Scott, also of Birmingham, to form the Webley and Scott Revolver and Arms Company Ltd of Birmingham. Both companies had been making revolvers for some years and had decided to pool resources. In 1920 it became illegal to own a pistol in Britain without a license, and sales fell. Webley continued to make revolvers for the army, but increasingly manufactured air pistols and air rifles. In 1979 the manufacture of firearms ceased entirely, and in 2008 its manufacture of air guns was moved to Turkey.

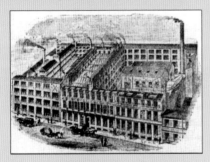

Webley & Scott factory located in Birmingham's Gun Quarter, c. 19th century

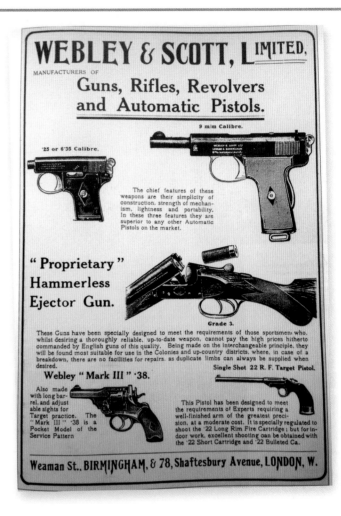

WEBLEY MARK IV

The Webley Mark IV, launched in 1898, saw the Webley revolver achieve its classic shape and mechanism. Like all Webleys, it fired a .455 cartridge from a six-round cylinder and was a double-action revolver. The MkIV featured an automatic extractor so that when the frame was opened, breaking down around a hinge under the front of the cylinder, a mechanism pushed all the cartridges up and out, greatly speeding up the business of reloading.

Webley logo

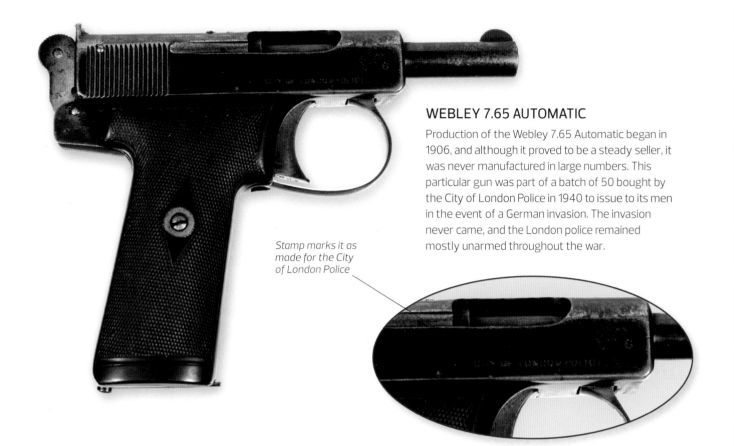

WEBLEY 7.65 AUTOMATIC

Production of the Webley 7.65 Automatic began in 1906, and although it proved to be a steady seller, it was never manufactured in large numbers. This particular gun was part of a batch of 50 bought by the City of London Police in 1940 to issue to its men in the event of a German invasion. The invasion never came, and the London police remained mostly unarmed throughout the war.

Stamp marks it as made for the City of London Police

WEBLEY MARK VI

The Webley Mark VI was introduced in 1915 with wider chambers to take new cartridges containing nitrocellulose propellant. It was manufactured in huge numbers, making this the most familiar of all the Webley models. This particular example has been rechambered to take .22 ammunition, not the standard .455. It was used for training junior officers in pistol shooting during their basic training.

Cylinder rechambered to fire .22 cartridges

Weapons of Espionage

Those of us who watch spy movies or films featuring glamorous secret agents are accustomed to seeing a host of gadgets and weapons that appear to stretch technology beyond the bounds of reason. The shadowy world of the real agents and spies, however, has produced a number of devices and weapons that are as equally bizarre and inventive as their fictional counterparts. Many of these weapons of espionage were made during World War II and the Cold War period that followed.

GAS GUN

This device is about the size and shape of a pen. It fires a small canister of tear gas and was intended to temporarily disable an opponent. The Lake Erie Chemical Corporation patented this gadget in 1932, marketing it to police forces and prison guards, but it also found its way into clandestine circles.

PEN-GUN

Disguised as a pen, this pistol from World War II is really a single-shot weapon firing a .22 caliber round that shows that the pen is indeed mightier than the sword! It is cocked by pulling back on the clip, and then fired by pushing on the button on the side of the device.

Chamber taking a .22 round

TOOL-GUNS

Apparently harmless little tools to be carried by any workman or mechanic, the tire gauge and screwdriver seen here are both small pistols firing .22 ammunition. They were supplied to Allied operatives dropped into occupied Europe during World War II.

.22 round discharged from here

Trigger and cocking mechanism

THE RESISTANCE

When German armed forces occupied France, Belgium, the Netherlands and Norway, nearly everyone expected it to be a merely temporary situation. The all-conquering German armed forces would quickly pummel Britain into surrender, whereupon the Germans would impose peace treaties, annex border territories and go home again. It was not until 1941 that people in the occupied countries began to realize that German occupation was going to last a lot longer, and be far more brutal, than they had envisaged.

Slowly resistance groups began to form. Some were nonviolent propaganda organizations, but increasingly those resisting German occupation turned to violence. The Allies were determined to help the resistance, sending them weapons, advice and personnel when possible.

An American officer and a French partisan join forces during a street fight in France, 1944.

THE LIBERATOR

Dubbed the "Liberator" to make it sound effective, this little pistol was officially named the FP45 M1942. The basic idea came from a Polish officer who had escaped the German invasion and thought that a small, cheap pistol would be useful to those operating behind German lines. Detailed design work was undertaken by George Hyde of General Motors, and the weapon went into production in summer 1942.

This was one of the simplest and cheapest pistols ever to enter mass production. It had only 23 parts, nearly all of which could be stamped out, with the barrel being turned. Just 300 workers produced more than a million of these little guns in just six weeks.

It was a crude weapon, able to fire a single .45 caliber cartridge. The barrel was smooth bore and short, so its effective range was only 25 feet.

It was intended as a personal protection weapon of last resort, fired to disable an enemy while the agent made a run for safety. Many thousands were distributed to occupied Europe, but few survived Liberators the war. They were so cheap and ineffective that they were often just thrown away. Today they are valuable collectors items.

Hollow butt can store ten rounds

Sliding sheet-metal cover prevents rounds falling out

PIPE-PISTOL

Apparently a smoking pipe, there is a gun secreted in the stem. The mouthpiece has to be removed for loading and firing, with the trigger being the knob on the side.

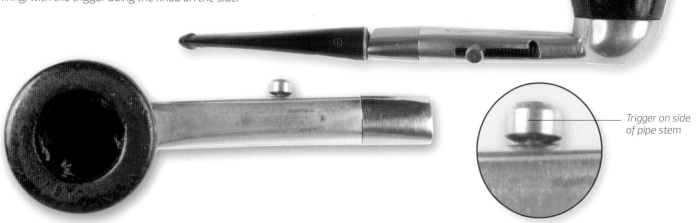

Trigger on side of pipe stem

THE COLD WAR

The term *cold war* was coined by British writer George Orwell when he wrote an article in October 1945 in which he predicted that the atomic bomb would make it effectively suicidal for any modern country to go to war again. He theorized that superpower rivalry would be played out by spies, business deals and diplomacy in a "cold war" that he contrasted with a "hot war," when armies marched to war. Before long it became clear that the Soviet Union and its communist satellites would be fighting just such a cold war against capitalist countries and Western democracies. The spies and secret agents of both sides used a wide variety of gadgets and weapons in their clandestine activities.

The Cold War enlisted spies armed with both traditional weapons and high-tech gadgets. Fictional spy James Bond, a product of the era, relied on highly improbable gadgetry along with his Walther.

LOZENGE-CASE GUN

This little tin of throat lozenges is actually a small gun that was used by an Italian assassin to murder an American rival in Switzerland during World War II. When the tin is opened it reveals what appears to be a pack of lozenges packed in foil. In fact this masks the pistol underneath. Pushing on one of the "lozenges" fires the gun.

Lozenge strip disguising trigger

Concealed barrel

FLUTE-GUN

Disguising a gun as a mundane object is even more effective if the object is able to function as it is supposed to do. Made in 1965, this flute will play quite normally, but in fact it hides a .22 single-shot pistol. The trigger takes the form of an innocuous brass screw attached to one of the keys.

Brass screw trigger

BELT-BUCKLE PISTOL

This belt looks like a normal part of the kit of a Nazi Party official. The leather is of usual size and construction, while the belt carries the swastika inside a wreath, just like the official belts. The buckle, however, is slightly thicker than is usual, and hidden within it is a small .22 caliber pistol. As with most other concealed weapons, this is effective only at very short range, but the concealment would allow the assassin to approach his victim without arousing suspicion.

Nazi swastika

Muzzle

.22 calber pistol hidden behind belt buckle

Hidden gun

PALM GUNS

Many agents active in the Cold War were issued with what were known as palm guns. These were tiny, easily concealed single-shot weapons that usually fired a small-caliber cartridge. They were generally intended as personal-defense weapons, though it is thought some may have been distributed for assassinations.

Gun unscrews for loading

Gun unscrews for loading

Shirt clip

RAZOR-PISTOL

Any everyday object that included a hollow tube in its construction could be used to hide a gun, with the barrel taking the place of the tube. This safety razor from the 1950s uses the handle to hide the barrel and firing chamber of a small pistol.

Handle unscrews to reveal gun barrel

ZIPPO LIGHTER—PISTOL

This genuine Zippo lighter has had its mechanism removed and replaced with what looks outwardly to be an identical contraption. In fact, what would normally be the gas outlet valve is a gun barrel, and a single-shot pistol is hidden in the container.

Muzzle

LIPSTICK-PISTOL

This highly decorative lipstick case conceals a tiny weapon designed for self-defense. This is an American version fired by twisting its knurled ring a quarter-turn. The most famous lipstick pistol was the KGB''s "kiss of death" for female agents, which contained a 4.5mm single-shot pistol encased in rubber.

Hidden gun

Post—World War II Pistols

Since the end of World War II there have been remarkably few major technological advances in handgun design, but that does not mean that today's weapons are identical to those of the 1940s. There have been significant advances in manufacturing techniques, which have had a profound influence on pistols and how they are used. Until the 1950s semiautomatic pistols were considerably more expensive than comparable revolvers. Their action was more complex and needed much more care and skill in

manufacture if they were not to jam or misfire with more regularity than was desirable.

Advancements in manufacturing during the 1950s and 1960s greatly improved the reliability of semiautomatics and reduced their price. By the 1970s many police forces had replaced revolvers with semiautomatics, and the military followed suit over the following decade and a half. In the 21st century revolvers are generally found only in private hands.

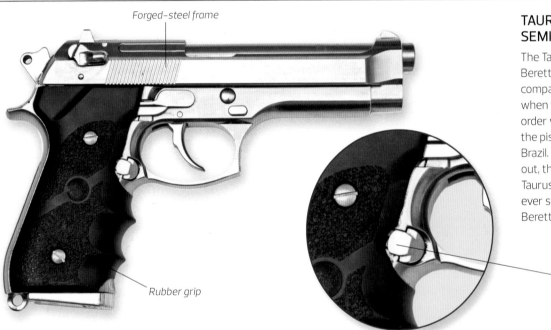

Forged-steel frame

Rubber grip

Magazine-release button

TAURUS PT92 SEMIAUTOMATIC PISTOL

The Taurus PT92 is a version of the Beretta 92 made by the Forjas Taurus company in Brazil. The gun originated when the Brazilian army placed a large order with Beretta for the Beretta 92, the pistols to be made under license in Brazil. When the Beretta patents ran out, the army sold the factory to Taurus, which has been making copies ever since. This model differs from the Beretta original in only minor ways.

SIG P226 SERVICE PISTOL

In 1984 the U.S. Army held trials to find a replacement for its ageing M1911 as a standard sidearm for officers. The contest was won by the Beretta 92F, partly on cost grounds; special forces, however, preferred the SIG P226 shown here. This pistol is manufactured by the German SIG Sauer company and can be chambered to fire a variety of cartridges. The pistol has spawned a wide range of variants, as police and armed forces around the world have placed orders for this pistol, each wanting slight changes for various reasons.

Butt holds eight-round removable magazine

PM (PISTOLET MAKAROVA) SEMIAUTOMATIC PISTOL

For many years the standard firearm of the Red Army, the Makarov PM Pistol is a straight blowback semiautomatic pistol. There is no locked breech in the Makarov; instead the barrel and breech are held in place only by the recoil spring. This gives a simple action that is easy to make and rarely malfunctions, but does necessitate a heavier breech to allow it to remain closed until the bullet has exited the barrel.

Makarov PM variation with brown grip

RUSSIAN MAKAROV PM PISTOL

The Makarov PM pistol fires 9mm ammunition from an 8- or 12-round magazine. It entered service with the Red Army in 1951 and gradually replaced older pistols as they wore out. Although cheap to manufacture and having reasonable stopping power, this pistol proved to be relatively inaccurate and was really only ever a personal protection weapon. In 2003 the Russian army began replacing this gun and serviceable examples were sold off.

EASTERN EUROPEAN REVOLVER

This revolver dates from post World War II, but its exact origins are not clear. Revolver design by then was fairly universal: it is of a generic design for a six-shot revolver and is of robust construction. It may have been made in Eastern Europe.

Cylinder holds six rounds of ammunition

Vent holes for combustion gases released within barrel

"Microject" rocket

GYROJET PISTOL

In the early 1960s, Americans Robert Mainhardt and Art Biehl developed one of the most unusual and innovative firearms of recent decades: the Gyrojet pistol. Instead of firing a bullet from a conventional cartridge, the Gyrojet fired a miniature "microjet" rocket that continued to accelerate after it left the barrel. Because the gun did not need to withstand the explosive power of a cartridge blasting a bullet along the barrel, it could be made of a very light zinc alloy. Ingenious though the system was, it failed to become popular partly due to the high cost of the ammunition and partly because of the low accuracy of the projectiles. MBA Associates, the company Mainhardt and Biehl set up to manufacture the weapon, also produced a carbine version.

No removable magazine (rounds pushed down from open "bolt")

3D PRINTED GUNS

The 3D printer is an industrial machine that is able to make a 3D shape of almost any size, shape or complexity by copying a digitally encoded design of an original object. The printer works by laying down successive layers of a material that dries or sets before the next layer is put down. Plastic, polymer and paper are the most common materials used, though some expensive industrial 3D printers can lay down certain types of metallic compounds.

In May 2013 Defense Distributed, an online organization that designs firearms, announced that they had produced digitized templates to allow a functioning pistol to be manufactured by anyone with a 3D digital printer capable of handling the specialized polymers required. The U.S. government immediately banned the company from distributing the software. The legal status of weapons made in this way is unclear and it is thought that most countries will soon pass legislation to restrict their manufacture and use.

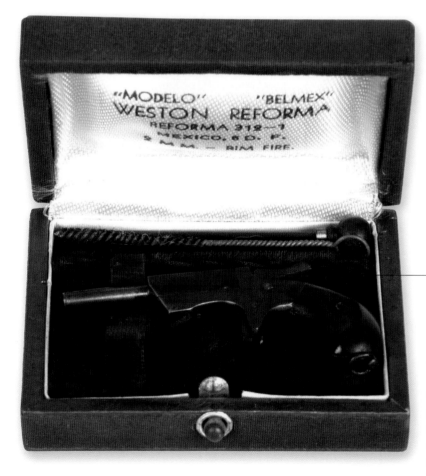

U.S. penny to indicate scale of Weston pistol

2¼ inch Belmex rimfire pistol

WESTON MINIATURE

Since the 1950s there has been a growing interest among collectors in miniature versions of antique or traditional pistols. The pioneer of the movement was Tom Weston, an American living in Mexico City in the 1950s who used local craftsmen to make working miniatures. Generally speaking, a firearm is considered a miniature only if it is one-third the size of the original, or smaller, and has all the correct working actions. This example is a miniature version of the Reforma single-shot pistol produced by Tom Weston.

BERETTA 92FS SEMIAUTOMATIC PISTOL

The Beretta 92 was adapted to military use as the M9, but the civilian version was itself improved to become the 92FS shown here. A key change was that the hammer has been enlarged compared to earlier models and fits behind the slide. The reason for this was that a few slides cracked after excessive use and then flew off backward when next fired. Other changes included an improved anti-corrosion coating and changes to the rifling of the barrel.

BERETTA M9 SEMIAUTOMATIC PISTOL

When the U.S. Army was looking for a new standard issue pistol in the 1980s it organized a series of trials and competitions that were won by the Beretta 92. After a few minor changes requested by the U.S. government, the pistol became the Beretta M9. The pistol fires 9 x 19mm ammunition from a 15-round magazine and is accurate to about 55 yards. The pistol began entering service in 1990 and remains the main U.S. Army pistol.

Slide-mounted safety catch

WALTHER P99 SEMIAUTOMATIC PISTOL

It took three years to design the P99, starting in 1994, with continual refinements being brought in to satisfy the German police forces who were the main intended customers. The 1997 version shown here was the result. It was purchased by several German Länder for their local police.

In 2003, the P99 saw further changes. The Finnish police wanted a slide that was easier for left-handed users to operator and a larger trigger guard to accommodate gloved fingers. When those changes were introduced, the Finns and Poles also bought the pistol. Further external modifications have been made since, but the internal workings have remained the same since 1997.

P99 variation with green polymer frame and grip

DESERT EAGLE

The Desert Eagle has gained a degree of fame and notoriety through its use in movies, computer games and TV shows, in which it is featured as one of the most advanced and powerful handguns available on the civilian market. Magnum Research, a specialist company based in Minnesota that produces custom and customized firearms, developed the gun. It entered production in 1982, and it has since undergone continuous upgrading and redesign. It can be chambered for a variety of ammunitions and incorporates a variety of custom features—one of the most popular of which is a coating of titanium nitride that results in a striped pattern like that of a tiger skin.

GLOCK 17 DUTY PISTOL

The Glock Safe Action Pistol was introduced in 1982 as a polymer framed, short recoil semiautomatic pistol. At first it did not sell well, as users worried a "plastic" frame would lack the durability and ruggedness of a metal frame. Those worries proved to be unfounded and this is now one of the most popular models of handgun in the world. The model shown here is the Glock 17 chambered to take 9 x 19mm cartridges.

Finger grooves on the front strap of the pistol grip

KEL-TEC PF-9 SEMIAUTOMATIC PISTOL

Released into the market in fall 2006, the Kel-Tec PF-9 is a 9mm recoil-operated, locked-breech, double-action semiautomatic pistol. With a claim that it is the flattest and lightest 9-mm pistol ever mass-produced, it is designed as a concealment and backup weapon for law enforcement and for civilian concealed carry.

Under-barrel accessory rail

HECKLER & KOCH USP

The USP (*Universale Selbstladepistole* or "universal self-loading pistol") is a gun sold to the civilian market, primarily in the United States. It incorporates a number of features developed by Heckler & Koch when that company competed in the 1991 contest to gain the contract to supply the U.S. special forces. Among these features is the lightweight polymer frame, the squeeze-cocking system and the delayed-blowback action. The pistol is available in 10 variants to civilians, plus a special Law Enforcement Modification (LEM) and other military versions.

Accessory rail at the front of the frame allows for attachments like laser sights and weapon lights.

HECKLER & KOCH MP7A1

Designed to fire 4.6 x 30mm ammunition that provides penetration approaching that of an assault rifle round, the MP7A1 is able to defeat the types of body armor frequently found in the hands of terrorists and criminal gangs. Designated a personal-defense weapon, it is smaller than a conventional submachine gun, and is can be carried and fired like a handgun. Several of the world's leading special operations units have adopted the MP7A1, including the U.S. Navy SEALs.

DEATH OF OSAMA BIN LADEN

That handheld firearms can still be essential to combat was shown by events on May 2, 2011, when U.S. Navy SEAL personnel launched a raid on the compound of wanted terrorist Osama bin Laden.

The attackers were armed with Heckler & Koch 416 carbine military assault rifles and Heckler & Koch MP7 pistols. The troops were landed by helicopter and the walls of the compound breached with explosive charges, then the troops attacked. One of the men in the compound opened fire with an AK478 from a balcony and the U.S. SEALs returned fire, continuing to fire as they entered the main house and moved from floor to floor. Bin Laden was shot dead in his bedroom, apparently as he reached for his Makarov pistol. In all, five people were killed, but most noncombatants were left uninjured. The use of personal firearms for the mission had allowed bin Laden to be killed with a minimum of collateral casualties.

About the Berman Museum

Since the Berman Museum of World History opened its doors to the public in April of 1996, thousands of visitors have enjoyed its unique and varied collection of art, historical objects, and weapons. Located in the Appalachian foothills in Anniston, Alabama, U.S.A., and next door to the 75-year-old Anniston Museum of Natural History, which is affiliated with the Smithsonian, the Berman Museum's reputation and collection have grown exponentially since its inception. The Berman Museum's holdings number 8,500 objects and it has 3,000 items related to world history exhibited in its galleries. Among the many rare and fascinating objects from around the world, there are items such as an air rifle from Austria, military insignia from German and Italy, a scimitar from the Middle East, and graphically carved kris holders from Indonesia. The Museum attracts both a global and regional audience. All who visit can appreciate the historic significance of the collection and gain greater awareness and respect of other cultures.

Its five galleries—Deadly Beauty, American West, World War I, World War II, and Arts of Asia—exhibit items spanning a period of 3,500 years. A focal point of the Deadly Beauty gallery is the elaborate Royal Persian Scimitar, circa 1550, created for Abbas the Great, King of Persia. The American West gallery covers approximately 200 years (c. 1700–1900), emphasizing the United State's political, economic, social, and cultural structures, and their influences on settling the West.

The World War galleries use objects from the Museum collection to explore the causes and conditions of both wars, the historical significance of the countries involved, and the resulting political, economic, cultural, and social changes brought about by each war.

A rare piece of equipment in the World War I gallery is the Tanker's Splinter Goggles, used by tank personnel to protect their eyes and faces from metal splinters from machine-gun fire. Exhibited in the World War II gallery is the M1942 "Liberator" Pistol, as well as a large collection of Adolf Hitler's tea and coffee service, purported to have come from the last bunker that the Führer occupied. The Arts of Asia exhibit features an extensive and ever-growing collection of Asian textiles, ceramics, sculpture, jade, and metal.

The Berman Museum of World History is home to the vast and eclectic collection of Colonel Farley L. Berman and his wife, Germaine. Farley Berman, a lifelong resident of Anniston, Alabama, served in the European theater during World War II, and in the occupation force afterward. There he met Germaine, a French national. They were married and spent the next 50 years traveling the world acquiring historic weapons and artifacts, paintings, bronzes, and other works of art. Berman's self-trained collector's eye recognized the importance of items that were perhaps seen as ordinary, and he made it his mission to preserve a few. The Bermans established contacts—and a reputation—in numerous auction houses and among antique dealers in Europe and America.

The Bermans freely shared their collection with the public long before the City of Anniston constructed the Museum facility. Hundreds of military dignitaries and others were invited to their home for personal tours of their collection. Colonel Berman could best be described as a colorful storyteller and was notorious for firing blank rounds from his collection of spy weapons when guests least expected. He advised aspiring collectors to purchase good reference books, spend some years reading, and visit a range of museums before acquiring.

During the early 1990s, several large museums expressed interest in receiving the Bermans' collection. They were disappointed when Germaine proposed that the collection remain in Anniston. Colonel and Mrs. Berman's collection stands as the core of Berman Museum. Since the Museum's opening, many have recognized its importance and have contributed their own personal treasures to this impressive collection.

BERMAN MUSEUM OF WORLD HISTORY

www.bermanmuseum.org
840 Museum Drive, Anniston, AL 36206

mail: P.O.Box 2245, Anniston, AL 36202-2245 USA
phone: +1-256-237-6261

Glossary

A

action Generally speaking, the overall firing mechanism of a gun

arquebus Shoulder-fired matchlock musket

B

ball A synonym for bullet, usually used before metal cartridges became common

barrel The metal, cylindrical part of a firearm through which the bullet travels.

bayonet A short knife-like weapon that can be attached to the muzzle of a firearm for use in hand-to-hand combat

blunderbuss A short, smoothbore musket with a flared muzzle, usually firing buckshot rather than a single ball. Sometimes used to refer to the weapon more properly called a dragon (q.v.)

bolt The part of a gun's action that, in a bolt-action gun, is pulled back to open the breech

bolt-action A gun (typically a rifle) whose action is operated by manipulating a bolt, either by drawing it back ("straight pull") or on a rotational axis

buckshot Lead pellets fired by shotguns, also called "shot"

butt, or buttstock The part of a gun braced against the shoulder for firing

C

caliber The diameter of a cartridge, expressed in fractions of an inch (e.g., .38, .45) or millimeter (e.g., 7.62mm, 9mm)

carbine A short-barreled, compact musket or rifle, originally carried by mounted troops or, in modern times, by soldiers whose primary jobs (vehicle crews, for example) made it impractical to carry a full-size rifle

cartridge The cased combination of bullet, powder and primer used in modern firearms; prior to the introduction of the metallic cartridge, the term referred to bullet and powder wrapped in paper for ease of loading muzzle-loading weapons

centerfire A type of cartridge with the primer sealed in a cavity in the center of its base

chamber The part of a gun in which the cartridge is seated before firing

clip A metal strip holding a number of cartridges for insertion into a gun

cock *See* dog

D

Darra gun A gun produced by the gunsmiths of Darra Adem Khel (formerly part of India, now part of Pakistan)

deringer The original weapon made by Henry Deringer; the imitation was spelled with an additional "r"

derringer Short, extremely compact and concealable pistol

dhal A Persian shield

dog The part of a flintlock mechanism that holds the flint

double-action A pistol (either revolver or automatic) in which a single, long trigger pull both fires the weapon and brings a cartridge into the chamber in readiness for firing; *see also* single-action

double-barrelled Having two barrels mounted side by side

dragon A pistol-like weapon with a smooth bore that fires buckshot, not a single bullet

dragoon A type of cavalry unit, so named as they were originally armed with dragons (*q.v.*)

F

firing pin The part of a gun's firing mechanism that strikes the cartridge's primer

flintlock Gun-firing system utilizing a piece of flint striking against a piece of steel to strike sparks for ignition

frizzon The part of a flintlock that the flint strikes to create sparks

G

gas-operated Term used to describe a gun that taps excess gas from the weapon to operate the action

gonne An obsolete word for a firearm of any kind

grip General term for the handle of a pistol

H

hammer The part of a modern firearm that strikes the cartridge and fires the gun

handgun Originally used to refer to any firearm that could be carried and used by an individual; in modern usage it refers solely to pistols

howdah pistol A powerful British pistol used by elephant riders to fend off tigers

J

jam A relatively common malfunction of firearms when a cartridge becomes jammed in the firing chamber and so prevents a new cartridge from being loaded

K

katana Traditional sword of the Japanese samurai

L

lever–action A gun that uses a lever, pushed downward and then upward by the firer, to load and eject cartridges

M

magazine The part of a gun containing cartridges in readiness for firing

matchlock Early firearms that used a slow–burning match to provide ignition

miquelot A form of flintlock popular in the Mediterranean area

musket Generally, a smoothbore, shoulder–fired infantry weapon, in use in the West up until the widespread introduction of rifles in the mid–19th century

muzzle The opening of a gun's barrel

muzzle–loading Used to refer to a gun that loads by the muzzle

P

pan The part of a flintlock in which priming powder *(q.v.)* is placed

pan cover The part of a flintlock mechanism that covers the pan and prevents priming powder from blowing away in wind

partisan A person fighting in a war who is not part of a recognized national army, but who claims allegiance to a national state

percussion cap A capsule containing a fulminating agent

pinfire An early type of self–contained cartridge, no longer in common use

polymer A material made up of large, complex molecules, specifically forms of plastic

primer The part of a cartridge which, when struck by the firing pin, ignites and fires the main charge

priming powder A small amount of gunpowder used in flintlocks, wheel locks and similar weapons to catch the sparks from the mechanism and detonate the main charge inside the barrel

pump–action A gun whose action is operated by a sliding mechanism, usually mounted below the barrel

pyrite A mineral that will create sparks when struck with steel, used for this purpose in wheel–lock weapons

R

ram A rod of metal or wood used to push the charge and bullet down the barrel of a muzzle–loading firearm.

receiver Generally speaking, the part of a gun incorporating the action, as distinct from the stock and barrel

recoil The backward pressure exerted when a gun is fired

recoil–operated A type of semi– or fully automatic gun that uses recoil to operate the action

revolver A firearm, usually a pistol, that can fire multiple rounds without reloading by revolving a cylinder to bring a new cartridge into line with the barrel

rifling The process of boring cylindrical grooves into a gun barrel to stabilize the bullet in flight, thus increasing accuracy

rimfire A type of cartridge in which the primer is evenly distributed around the rear of the base

round Synonym for cartridge, usually used to refer to magazine capacity, e.g., 20–round.

S

safety The part of a gun's action designed to prevent accidental firing

self–loading *See* semiautomatic

semiautomatic Used to refer to guns that will fire once with each trigger pull without the need to reload; the term is synonymous with *self–loading*

shotgun Smoothbore, shoulder–fired weapon, typically firing buckshot; most commonly used in hunting but also in combat

single–action A revolver that has to be manually cocked before each shot; single–action automatics require cocking only before the first shot is fired; *see also* double–action

smoothbore A gun with an unrifled barrel; *see* rifling

snaphance, snaphaunce A type of lock, an ancestor of the flintlock

stock Any part of a gun that is gripped with the hand before firing, e.g., forestock; *see also* butt

T

torador A matchlock musket that was used in India for hundreds of years

trigger The part of a gun's action pulled back by the firer's finger to discharge the weapon

trigger guard A part of the gun's frame that goes around the trigger to prevent an accidental knock pushing the trigger and so firing the gun

W

wheel lock Firing mechanism that used the friction of a spring–powered metal wheel against iron or flint for ignition

Index

Acknowledgments

Moseley Road Inc would like to thank the following people for their assistance and patience in the making of this book: The Berman Museum of World History: Adam Cleveland, David Ford, Susan Doss, Evan Prescott, Sara Prescott, Quinton Turner and Kira Tidmore; and Lisa Purcell for being creative under intense pressure.

Picture Credits

Unless otherwise noted, all silhouetted weaponry images are from the Berman Museum of World History, Anniston, Alabama, and photographed by *f*-stop fitzgerald and Jonathan Conklin Photography, Inc., with the exception of the following:

KEY : *t* = top; *c* = center; *b* = bottom; *l* = left; *r* = right; *p* = panel

Cover *t* Creative HQ/Shutterstock; cover *b* mj007/Shutterstock; 6*bl* Stadtbibliothek Nürnberg/Public Domain; 6*tl* Hatchetfish/Wikimedia Commons; 7*t* zimand/shutterstock; 7*b* Trulock/Wikimedia Commons; 8 Daderot/Wikimedia Commons; 9*t* r.classen/shutterstock; 9*m* mikeledray/shutterstock; 9*b* joppo/shutterstock; 19*b* 0–11 Hitdelight/Shuttterstock; 12 *The Battle of Grandson* by Diebold Schilling/Public Domain; 19*p Blackbeard in Smoke and Flames* by Frank E. Schoonover/ Public Domain; 23*p Surrender of General Burgoyne* by John Trumbull/Public Domain; 25*p Prince Rupert of the Rhine* by Simon Verelst/Public Domain; 27*p Rear-Admiral Sir Horatio Nelson, 1758–1805* by Lemuel Francis Abbott/Public Domain; 35*b* Balefire/Shutterstock; 36*b* Olga Popova/Shutterstock; 37*b* spaxiax/Shuttertock; 38*p Tipu, Sultan of Mysore* by Robert Laurie/Public Domain; 38*b* Zerbor/shutterstock; 39*t* Dimedrol68/shutterstock; 39*b* Zerbor/shutterstock; 41*p Duel between Burr and Hamilton*/Public Domain; 44*p Eugene Onegin and Vladimir Lensky's Duel* by Ilya repin/Public Domain; 42*c Hastings-Francis Duel* by A.D. Macromick/Public Domain; 45*c* Andras Vadas/Wikimedia Commons; 45*p Duke of Wellington v. Earl of Winchilsea* by Thomas Howell Jones/Public Domain; 56–57 mikeledray/shutterstock; 58 *The Pursuit*/Library of Congress; 61*t* Zerbor/shutterstock; 63*p Assassination of President Lincoln*/Library of Congress; 67*t Samuel Colt* by Gerald S. Hayward/Public Domain; 76*p* Public Domain; 76 *pb* Library of Congress; 77*t* Library of Congress; 80*p* National Portrait Gallery/Public Domain; 82*p Les dernières cartouches* by Alphonse-Marie-Adolphe de Neuville/Public Domain; 86 Library of Congress; 87*p* Library of Congress; 89*t* Rama/Wikimedia Commons; 89*bl* Olemac/shutterstock; 89*b* right Public Domain; 93*p* Public Domain; 94 Library of Congress; 95*t* Rama/Wikimedia Commons; 95*c* Mikoyan21/Wikimedia Commons; 95*p* Public Domain; 96*p* Library of Congress; 96*b* Rama/Wikimedia Commons; 98*c The Charge of the 21st Lancers at the Battle of Omdurman* by Richard Caton Woodville/Public Domain; 98*p* Imperial War Museum; 99*b* M62/Wikimedia Commons; 101*p* DeiMosz/shutterstock; 103*t Winter 1882* by Francesc Masriera/Public Domain; 112*cr* Bibliothèque nationale de France; 114–15 Dave Allen Photography/shutterstock; 116 National Library of Scotland; 118*b* Library of Congress; 120*p* Public Domain; 123*t* Public Domain; 124*bl* FBI; 125*p* Public Domain; 129*t* http://ww2db.com; 130*p* Public Domain; 132*pl* http://ww2db.com; 132*pc* German Federal Archive (Bundesarchiv); 135*p* Library of Congress; 136*p* Birmingham Gun Museum; 136*r* Birmingham Gun Museum; 140*p* Photoshot; 144*t* Vudhikrai/shutterstock; 144*b* Michael Coddington/shutterstock; 145*t* Tereshchenko Dmitry/shutterstock; 145*b* zimand/shutterstock; 148t Jaroslaw Grudzinski/shutterstock; 148b Vartanov Anatoly/shutterstock; 149t Mishella/shutterstock; 149t inset sirimiri/Wikimedia Commons; 149b Nomad_Soul/shutterstock; 150t zimand/shutterstock; 150b Photoexpert/Shutterstock; 151t Vartanov Anatoly/shutterstock; 151t *inset* Bobbfwed/Wikimedia Commons; 151b KrisfromGermany/Wikimedia Commons; 153 Hitdelight/Shuttterstock